Internet Income Explained

How to Launch an Online Business in 48 Hours
Even if You Have No Products, No Service,
or No Idea Where to Start

Keala Kanae

Internet Income Explained

How to Launch an Online Business in 48 Hours Even if You Have No Products, No Service, or No Idea Where to Start

Keala Kanae

ISBN Paperback: 978-1-962280-25-9

ISBN Ebook: 978-1-962280-24-2

HERE'S A GIFT BEFORE YOU EVEN BEGIN!

To say thanks for getting my book, here's a bonus gift to help you take action and get results quickly.

What if you could sell the exact same products we've earned more than $100M selling? What if we gave you the exact same sales funnels we've used to sell those products? What if we even gave you a proven follow up sequence (i.e. emails) to turn your leads into customers? Well, that's exactly what you get when you unlock our Vertical Selling System™.

Go to iiexplained.com to get all the juicy details and jump start your business today!

Contents

Part 1

Offers

Chapter 1

Imagine…

I want you to imagine for a moment a lifestyle that's most likely completely different from the one you're living right now. Imagine yourself traveling to places most people will never see. You stay in the most beautiful hotels and drink the finest wines. You take a third of your year off whenever you want, and your income grows substantially *while you are on vacation.*

That is my reality, thanks to the skills I teach in this book. Last year, I took a total of four months off throughout the year, and yet my income grew by about 121%.

See, most people trade time for money, but the wealthy trade money for time. And what most of us experience as a cap on our income is actually a cap on the number of hours we can work, disguised as an income ceiling. If you could decouple time and money as I have done, what would life be like for you?

This book teaches you a skill set that allows you to have both time and financial freedom. To date, I've earned over $100 million applying these skills, yet not that long ago, I was working in a coffee shop for minimum wage, with a credit score of about 530, and living in my mom's spare bedroom. I wasn't even living paycheck to paycheck—most of the time I ran out of money before the next payday. But within seven months of doubling down and taking massive action on the skills that you're about to learn, I achieved my first $10,000 month. I quit that coffee shop job and haven't looked back since.

I wrote this book to help you start a freelance marketing business from scratch that works *even if you've never started an online business before.* It doesn't matter if you're sixteen or sixty, I have seen these skills work for people of all age brackets, backgrounds, and ethnic groups. I've even seen it work for people who barely speak English, and people who had no prior experience as an entrepreneur. I believe that if you apply the skills in this book, you can see similar results for yourself or greater. In fact, you could get 90% of the process wrong and still become a millionaire.

Years ago I worked as a server at a fine restaurant, where I occasionally had tables of guests who would order $1,000 or even $1,500 bottles of wine. One night, some of our customers started ordering $750 shots. I remember thinking to myself, "*Who in the world can afford to spend a thousand bucks on a couple of drinks with dinner?*"

My coworkers would even make fun of those guests. "Look at the douchebag at table number seventy-six with his $1,000 bottle of wine!"

Today, I *am* that douchebag.

Joking aside, I *have* been able to drink some of the finest wines in the world. I recently indulged in a cognac that was 150 years old and made from a grape that is now extinct. I have eaten some of the finest foods made by some of the most famous chefs at restaurants where your average tab is over $1,000 and the reservation wait list is eight months long. I've been able to see parts of the world that most people will only ever see as a picture on a calendar or on the movie screen.

Most importantly, I've been able to do it all without taking time off of work, asking for vacation time from a boss, or needing approval from any other authority—all while watching my income grow. While some might label me a douchebag because of the luxury lifestyle I can afford today, if I had to choose, I wouldn't go back.

So take a moment to imagine if *you* had the freedom and flexibility to have dominion over your destiny. Imagine if you had a set of skills that allowed you to have complete control over your financial future, and no longer needed to trade your time for money. Where would you go? What places would you choose to see in the world? What people would you choose to spend time with?

I recently heard a success story from one of my clients, Sarah, whose mother was diagnosed with terminal cancer. Sarah immediately took time away from her business and spent every day of her mom's last four months of life by her side.

"Last month I made $15,000 and I barely worked," she told me during a recent conversation. "I don't even know what I would do if I hadn't met you."

For most of us, taking four months off of work to be with someone we love during their last days of life is simply not an option. Most of us do not have that freedom. That's why I say that this is about more than just *your* life—it's about the lives of all of the people that you love most. Like Sarah's mother, our loved ones are the secondary beneficiaries of our learning these skills. Who in your life would be impacted by this change?

I recently read a book called *Stealing Fire: How Silicon Valley, the Navy SEALs, and Maverick Scientists Are Revolutionizing the Way We Live and Work,* by Steven Kotler and Jamie Wheal. The authors mention a study on people diagnosed with a terminal illness who had a substantial chance of saving their own lives if they were willing to change certain habits. The researchers found that only 15% of people could change their habits when their lives were at stake.

That means *85% of people will die before they will change their habits.*

Think about that for a moment. What greater price could somebody pay for their habits than death? If you're not willing to change your habits to ensure you live a long, healthy life, what do you think the odds are that you're going to change your habits just to make money?

Metaphorically speaking, it's possible to "die" in your twenties but live into your eighties. In other words, you can end up droning through your life on autopilot, never truly alive, trapped in circumstances that don't allow you to reach your full potential. Are you going to be among the 15% who change or the 85% who die, even if only metaphorically? You should decide right now which side of that line you want to be on.

One thing that tips the scales in your favor is to realize that there's more at stake than just you and your resistance to change. It's not just about your ability to change—it's about the change that happens for everyone else in your life *because* you changed. You see, most people will not change to save themselves, but they will do it to save those they love. Everybody in your life will be impacted by the information and skills in this book, even if you are the only one to read it.

My fiancé, Tiani, lives a completely different life today than she did when we first met. My mom lives a completely different life today than she did a decade ago when I was struggling at my minimum-wage job. And everyone who works for my company will tell you that their lives have changed as a result of the skills contained in this book, even if indirectly.

How? I take my team traveling twice a year to places they never would have been able to afford to visit. I've treated them to fine wines and meals at some of the best restaurants in the world. We have given them large cash rewards—in fact, one of our hard-working team members recently paid off $35,000 of debt leftover from her divorce. She doesn't know it yet, but at the end of this year (2023), we're going to give her that $35,000 back in the form of a check, because we saw how hard she worked to make that happen for herself and her son. I learned and mastered these skills, and today, everyone around me benefits because of it.

Most people talk about doing good things for their families, their communities, and the world. But the ability to do that starts by doing good things for yourself. You fill no cups when yours is empty. When an oxygen mask falls out of the ceiling in an aircraft, they tell you to put yours on first because you can't help anyone else until you are okay. Until you are wealthy, you cannot change the wealth of anybody else in your life. Likewise, when you struggle to make ends meet, others in your life can pay the price too.

In 2012, I was twenty-nine years old and earning minimum wage at a coffee shop in Honolulu, Hawaii, where I was born and raised. That wasn't even close to a livable wage in the priciest city in America. On August 13, 2012, I walked into my mom's bedroom while she was folding laundry, and I asked probably the most embarrassing question of my life.

"Hey Mom, do you still have that cardboard box that you were going to take down to Goodwill to donate?"

She turned around. "Yeah, I do, but what do you need it for?"

"Well, tomorrow is Tiani's birthday and I have no money to get her anything. I was hoping I could find something in that box to give her as a gift."

That day, I went shopping in a cardboard box to find my girlfriend a birthday gift. And on August 14, 2012, I gave Tiani somebody else's trash for her birthday.

As embarrassing as that story is, I'm grateful for that experience because it's the moment when I made the solemn oath, the undying commitment, to find a way out of that situation permanently. I was willing to go to any seminar, buy any course, read any book, and look under any rock necessary to make that happen because I realized that the people that I loved most were paying the price for how I was showing up in my life.

It's not that I hadn't attempted to improve my financial picture. For the twelve years prior to that moment, I had tried just about everything (I'm sure you can relate to this!). I joined almost every network marketing company that you can think of. I dragged friends and family to hotel meetings where we drew diagrams on a whiteboard roughly in the shape of a pyramid. All you had to do was get three people to sign up who would then get three people who would get three people...all of planet Earth would be in our downline at some point, and passive riches were sure to follow!

It didn't work. I tried door-to-door sales, cold calling, real estate, options trading, stocks—I even had some "extra-legal" businesses (Not *illegal* of course, because that would be bad! Wink.). I started a nightclub promotions business, and a clothing line—I even bought and flipped cars at one point. For twelve years straight, you name it, I did it. Until I finally stumbled upon the secret that I'm about to share with you inside this book.

It's called freelance marketing.

I actually discovered freelance marketing in 2010. At the time, I was promoting a real estate investment education program with a direct sales company, and I didn't have the ability to convince my friends and family to come with me to a seminar (because I had already done that so many damn times that everyone in my life had flagged me as *Do Not Answer* on their phones). I was in the NFL—No Friends Left—Club.

By the way, I sometimes make fun of network marketing, but I actually don't have anything against it. I've made a lot of money selling network marketing products, but not via the traditional route. Instead, I used the skills you'll learn in this book to sell so much product for a certain network marketing company in such a short amount of time that they had to change the compensation plan because I was driving so much volume. By applying the principles in this book, I single-handedly changed their business model.

But back to my story. One day, Nouveau Riche, the company whose real estate education products I was promoting, made an announcement: they had struck a deal with Realflow founder Greg Clement to use a new online tool that he had developed. Clement was using a simple landing page (essentially a one-page website) to bring real estate investment buyers and sellers from across the US together online, and he earned commissions from deals those buyers and sellers made together. To build his network of potential clients, he ran online advertisements to drive buyers and sellers to his landing page, where he offered a free eBook on real estate investing in exchange for their email addresses. Clement was running his massively successful business all from his kitchen table—pretty revolutionary back in 2010!

Clement agreed to provide his landing page templates to Nouveau Riche via subscription for about $100/month. When I logged into this new landing page tool for the first time, I realized that although this guy was doing deals across the country, his profits didn't involve knocking on doors, cold-calling prospects, or dragging friends and family to seminars. He simply got people to fill out a form, then connected buyers and sellers on the back end and took a sliver of commission from each deal.

I was intrigued! I couldn't afford $100 a month to subscribe to the landing page tool, so I went online and found a free web builder, Wix, and built my own landing page. I wrote my own eBook as a free downloadable gift and started putting ads on Craigslist to drive people to my site. I think I called my book something like *The Dirty Dozen: Twelve Real Estate Investing Secrets Nobody Wants You To Know.*

A few people downloaded the book in exchange for their name, email, and phone number. I picked up the phone and started calling people on my new list of contacts. On the first day, a woman answered.

I said, "Hi, this is Keala, and I'm calling because you downloaded my free book yesterday, and I was hoping to connect with you to see how serious you were about learning real estate investing."

She wigged out. "Wait, you're the guy who wrote the book? You're actually *calling* me? I can't believe you're calling me. I never expected you to do that!" Because I picked up the phone and called her personally, she was suddenly open to anything that I would have offered her at that point. In her mind, I had a position of authority simply because of the way we'd connected.

I was shocked. Before, when I cold-called people, I'd either been hung up on or told to F-off. But this lady was eating out of the palm of my hand.

There was a moment during that phone conversation where I literally pulled the phone away from my ear and just looked at it. When I told her about a free class coming up in her area, my pitch felt natural and easy. This was the moment when it hit me: "*Holy shit, this method is totally different from everything I've tried before!*"

In the end, she didn't buy anything from me, but that experience got me interested in the idea of an online business. I started to Google things like how to generate leads online, which took me down a rabbit hole of learning about freelance marketing. I started reading stories on forums about experts in the space who would take time away from their businesses to travel for half the year, but whose incomes would stay consistent. These people could work anywhere in the world as long as they had a WiFi connection. And, they built automated systems into their businesses that brought in money whether they were eating, sleeping, or on vacation. I had discovered the concept of passive income.

And I thought, "*Now* that *is the American dream.*" Not knocking on doors, dragging people to hotel meetings, or getting yelled at on the phone.

In September 2012, after two years of researching passive income methods and dabbling without making any real money, I doubled down and focused hard on implementing what I'd learned. By April 2013 I'd made my first five-figure month and was able to quit my coffee shop job. Six months after that, I was consistently bringing in $20,000 to $30,000 per month. Within about another year and a half, I was making six figures *per month*.

What made the difference in the two years when I went from making nothing to being so successful that my entire life changed?

It came down to two things:

1. I got committed
2. I got the right coaching and mentoring to learn the skills I needed to succeed.

Even though I couldn't afford it at the time, I sought out coaches and mentors who had the results I wanted to have, and I figured out a way to hire them to teach me. I attended a life-altering freelance marketing event in San Diego, even though I couldn't afford the plane ticket or cost of admission (I'll tell more of that story in the coming chapters). And I learned an important lesson:

We either pay the price of success or we pay the price of failure. Either way, there's a price. But eventually, the pain of not knowing how to execute what we learn becomes so great that we are willing to pay others to coach and mentor us so that we can shortcut trial and error. And that's when our lives begin to change.

This is why I wrote this book—to give you that shortcut to decoupling time and money. Listen, I'm here for both selfish and *selfless* reasons. I hope that reading this book is just the first step in your relationship with me and my team. I hope it makes you want to work with my company, to learn more from us, and let us coach and mentor you to master the skills that you will learn in the next chapters. But I also know that for some people, that may not be an option given current financial constraints. At this point, I've seen this information change thousands of lives through our company. So, this book is a way for me to get this information into as many hands as possible in the hope that I can make a difference in the world by sharing skills and a business roadmap that I know can work for you.

Listen, I have something to sell you, and I hope that you buy it. But not for my benefit. Whether or not you buy my products or services or work with my company one-on-one does not change my life at all. I'm still going to eat at the same restaurants, go on the same vacations, fly in the same private jets, live in the same house, and drive the same fancy cars. But *your* life could radically change if you choose to book a call with my team because they can help you accelerate your path to success.

I didn't write this book to change *my* life. I very much wrote it to change *yours*.

My sincere hope is that you take this book's information seriously. Do not look at this as just some other opportunity that you found on the internet, but instead, realize that the words on these pages are the keys to your dream life.

I hope that you will invest the time and energy, and make the commitment to master these skills—and in doing so, master your destiny.

Dear Reader, what if you could sell the exact same products we've earned more than $100M selling? What if we gave you the exact same sales funnels we've used to sell those products? What if we even gave you a proven follow up sequence (i.e. emails) to turn your leads into customers? Well, that's exactly what you get when you unlock our Vertical Selling System™. Go to iiexplained.com to get all the juicy details and jump start your business today!

Chapter 2

What Is Freelance Marketing and Why Is It Best for Beginners?

Freelance marketing is the business of selling someone else's products or services in exchange for a commission. As a business model, it is one of the best for beginners, especially in the online space.

It's no secret that many businesses fail early on because they're either not able to acquire customers or they're not able to make sales to those customers so that the business becomes profitable. In their Harvard Business Review article, "What Entrepreneurs Get Wrong," authors Vincent Onyemah, Martha Rivera Pesquera, and Abdul Ali explain:

> Salesmanship is central to the success of any young company, and entrepreneurs ignore this at their peril. Yet many do ignore it, in large part because they have little sales experience and have probably not taken classes in how to sell, even if they have formal business education.

Even trained sales professionals struggle to find prospects and close sales. According to the sales engagement platform SPOTIO, "More than 40% of salespeople say prospecting is the most challenging part of the sales process, followed by closing (36%) and qualifying (22%)."

Businesses can also fail because they grew too quickly—early on, I almost fell under the weight of my own success because my sales skyrocketed so fast. But I believe the majority of businesses fail because they can't acquire customers and build revenue quickly enough to sustain and exceed their expenses. Most entrepreneurs are amazing at delivering their products or services—they're just not very skilled in marketing and sales. That's why companies will happily pay a referral fee to freelance marketers who can help acquire new customers. As you will learn, you can build a multimillion-dollar business solving this problem for other businesses.

But first, let's talk about why you should start a business in the first place (instead of investing in some other sort of wealth-building strategy). In his Forbes article, "Why A Business Opportunity Might Be A Wise Investment," Rhett Kniep writes that businesses are a wiser (and safer) investment opportunity than things like the stock market, real estate and cryptocurrency. Why? Kniep writes:

> As a business advisor at a mergers and acquisitions firm, I believe a business opportunity is an often-overlooked investment, but one that can satisfy the "unknowns" so common to other investment opportunities. Foremost, however, the business investment is an investment in you as a person. It capitalizes on your direct input to create success. And ultimately, I believe the best investments are always investments in people.

Your freelance marketing business allows you to satisfy all the requirements of a successful business so long as you follow what you learn in this book. First, you can focus all your efforts on products and services that are in demand. Second, your business will always be what Kniep calls "improvable or innovative" because you are only limited by your own creativity—as you'll learn in Chapter 9 when we talk about how to create offers that can make you a millionaire. And third, your freelance marketing business is scalable. As you'll see in Chapter 8, once you set your business up and get it running smoothly, you'll have the power to 8X your income on demand (without much extra effort) by optimizing your sales and marketing.

Freelance marketing isn't a fly-by-night business model, by the way. So much of what is touted on the internet these days includes low-level tactics that may sound like new and intriguing opportunities but will not stand the test of time. The concept of paying somebody a referral fee for sending you a customer has been around since the beginning of commerce. Centuries ago, for example, kings would pay for referrals for professionals who could provide services to their royal court. It may look different today, but freelance marketing as a business model isn't going anywhere. In fact, you could spend the next several decades of your life building a business like this and still have a viable business model to pass on to your heirs.

This is also an enterprise-level business model, meaning multibillion-dollar companies have been launched off the back of the freelance marketing concept. Credit Karma is a great example of this. They have none of their own products or services—instead, they offer people free access to their credit reports via an easy-to-use app. When users sign up, Credit Karma collects user data that allows them to promote relevant products and services (i.e. credit cards, vehicle financing, and home mortgages) from third parties who pay Credit Karma a commission whenever a user signs up for one of their products. Credit Karma is literally just a freelance marketing business—albeit at an enterprise level with a massive budget. And it recently sold to Intuit for $7 *billion.*

Listen, I don't know if you're interested in becoming a billionaire with this business model. I'm just letting you know that you *could.* It's been done. I remember when I was working at the coffee shop for minimum wage, I just wanted to make ten grand a month and not have to report to somebody for eight to ten hours a day, or ask permission to use the restroom or take a week off of work so that I could enjoy some time with family. I just wanted more independence and a six-figure income so I could enjoy a comfortable standard of living. Wherever you're starting from or whatever your initial goal is, freelance marketing can support that goal; and if you follow the process I teach in this book, you won't have to worry about the rug being pulled out from you six to twelve months from now.

I want you to think about this strategically. You obviously want to be an entrepreneur—that's why you picked up this book, right? And arguably an entrepreneur's most important skill is the ability to acquire customers and sell to them. By becoming a freelance marketer first in your evolution as a business owner, you will stay narrowly focused on mastering the one skill set that is the Achilles' heel of most other entrepreneurs.

This was my first epiphany when I first considered this business model. I thought,

> *Okay, obviously I have a goal of being an entrepreneur and I don't necessarily want to be a freelance marketer for the rest of my life. But if someone else's business is going to take care of all of the inventory, shipping, hiring, firing, merchanting, refund requests, support tickets, customer hassles, legal drama, financials and all that stuff—and all I have to do to get paid is just send customers their way, then I will get really good at the one thing that most businesses suck at. And if I can just spend my time getting really good at that over the next few years, the options available to me as an entrepreneur will be tremendous!*

I knew I'd found something that would give me more opportunities than I could possibly capitalize on—which is exactly what happened. And it all started when I was walking down the street in San Diego and got a notification on my phone that I'd earned that first $25 commission I mentioned earlier. Not a lot of money, I admit, but I still remember every detail about that pivotal moment right down to the T-shirt I was wearing and the street I was walking down. It happened in September 2012 while I was attending my first freelance marketing event. That event is where I learned the freelance marketing principles that enabled me to change the trajectory of my life.

The crazy thing is, I almost missed the conference entirely. A few months prior, I had joined a community of online marketers to learn more about the business. One day while riding the city bus, I was listening to a conference call promoting the event. On the call were company founders and big-time marketers who were sharing success stories about how attending the previous year's event had changed their businesses, and how important it was for aspiring marketers to be there. They told about how they'd gone from earning $2,000 per month to $10,000 after attending. One person had even increased his sales from $10,000 to $50,000 in monthly revenue after implementing the strategies he'd learned.

I remember sitting on the bus listening in on this call and thinking to myself, *"Oh, sure, I'll go to your stupid event once you prove to me that this thing works."*

But suddenly, I realized, *"Wait a second. What if I'm looking at this all backward? What if I have to go to the event in order for the thing to work?"* It occurred to me that all of the people on the call had the results that I wanted to have, but rather than taking their advice, I was arguing with them about why it couldn't work for me! I had a flashback to all the times in my life when I'd ignored good advice. Where had that gotten me? Nowhere.

I had to get to this event.

As soon as I got home, I opened my laptop and checked my bank account: I had $40 to my name. The airfare alone would cost me at least $600! Still, I decided I was going to make it to San Diego no matter what. That night, I went through my closet and my mom's closet too. I pulled out everything we could get rid of—clothes, DVD players, all the stuff we didn't need—and listed everything for sale on Craigslist. The next day, I went to work and stuck a Post-it note on the refrigerator offering to pick up shifts for anybody who wanted extra time off in those next few weeks. When I got home I announced on Facebook that I was trying to come up with additional money to pay for an event I really wanted to attend. I wasn't looking for handouts, but if anyone had work they needed doing around the house, like moving furniture, painting, cleaning the yard, detailing a car or whatever, I was looking to pick up extra work.

Over the next three weeks, I earned enough money to buy a ticket to the event and airfare to San Diego. Great! Except…now I was broke again. That night, my girlfriend Tiani asked me where I was going to stay in California.

"Oh, shit!" I said. "I didn't think of that." I'd never traveled alone before as an adult, so it didn't even cross my mind to book a hotel. I told her that if worse came to worst, I'd just sleep at the convention center.

"Keala, you can't sleep at the convention center!"

There had to be a way for me to pay for this trip. At that point, I couldn't afford to keep living the way I was. I *had* to be there! We both remembered that one of our friends, who was in the Navy, had just been stationed in San Diego with his wife. I reached out to him, and it turned out that their new apartment was just a few miles from the convention center. They said I could sleep on their couch.

I swear on my life that if I hadn't had that couch to sleep on, I would have slept on the floor at the convention center and showered at the public change rooms at the beach right outside—that's how badly I wanted to go. Most people would not have made that kind of sacrifice. See, most people want change without pain. But there's no such thing. We've got to give up our comfort if we want to achieve new heights. For me, sleeping outside of a convention center for three days was a minor price to pay for the life-changing experience that marketing event turned out to be.

While I was in San Diego, I earned that first $25 commission as a freelance marketer. Fast forward to late 2015—just three years later—and I had already made a million dollars using the same business model. People kept asking me how I was getting such life-changing results, so I began selling my own products online to teach others what I knew. First, I sold a course about Facebook advertising and another one on copywriting. By November 2016, I had launched my own in-depth course and coaching business, now known as Fullstaq Marketer. And four months after launch, we were bringing in over a million dollars a month in revenue.

I am proof that you can learn these skills and that once you learn to find clients and make sales, the opportunities are endless. You can apply the skills you learn in this book to any business, not just freelance marketing. These skills are key to the success my companies experience today. As I write this book in the fall of 2023, we've made over $100 million in sales so far this year. I have partnerships with six additional companies, and am in the due diligence stage of buying two more companies. I didn't get here overnight, but where I am today in life would not have been possible without the skills you'll learn right here in this book.

I think it's important to point out that in a lot of ways, freelance marketers actually make *more* profit than other company owners. On average you can earn commissions of 30% to 50% of a sale for most offers that exist online. I've even seen offers where you can earn 70% to 75%. And I've seen offers where you earn *100%* of every sale that you make. Those are rare, but to be extra conservative, it's safe to say that on average you will take home 30% of the revenue that you generate for another business.

Most entrepreneurs—I'm talking 98% of them—are not taking home 30% of the revenue that their business is bringing in. And they have all of the additional headaches of hiring and firing employees, dealing with legal issues, financial challenges, balance sheets, PNLs, employees stealing money or hours, customer complaints and refunds, and poor reviews on the BBB. And then you have to consider the toll on their time, their families, and the stress they endure—all to make less money per unit than a freelance marketer.

Actually, there are many days that I question whether or not I made the right decision to go from freelance marketer to full-fledged entrepreneur. A few years ago I had a company that was losing money for an entire year—I worked so hard but made nothing. There were times when I thought, *"Goddamn, why am I doing this?"* Once you've grown a freelance marketing business, you may never feel the need to expand into any other enterprise. But if you do, the skill set you'll learn will give you a huge advantage as an entrepreneur, and you'll always have the freelance marketing model to fall back on should you need it.

Let's look at the core skill set that we will cover in the coming chapters:

1. **Media buying**: The skill of placing advertisements online in front of the right audience who are most likely to buy your product or service. This is a massively valuable skill—I have friends who are deca-millionaires and their only skill is media buying.
2. **Copywriting**: The skill of convincing someone to buy something via the written word through an advertisement, email, sales letter, or online presentation like a webinar.
3. **Funnel design**: Knowing how to design web pages or simple websites purely to optimize sales conversions.
4. **How to turn any audience into money.** Leveraging social media, email, and webinars to make a profit.
5. **Email list management**: How to attract subscribers to join your email list so you can monetize it with your affiliate offers.
6. **Persuasion and influence:** Showing your audience how your product or service will make a meaningful difference in their life, resulting in them making the decision to buy.

Of all the skills that I've learned over the years, persuasion and influence are easily the most valuable. I use them every day: in my relationship with my fiancé, in managing my team, in my marketing and sales material, and when building a great culture in my companies. I've devoted several YouTube videos to talking about how I use these skills on a daily basis, and I've been interviewed on several podcasts to talk about how important these overarching skills are to every facet of my life.

You'll notice I didn't include team management in my list of key skills you'll learn as a freelance marketer, and that's because the majority of freelance marketers can run this business model by themselves. Granted, I did bring on a couple of team members toward the end of my career as a freelance marketer when I was transitioning into coaching and product sales. And I know a few freelancer marketers who have small teams (under five people). You might outsource certain aspects of your business for things like video edits or graphics, but you won't need a lot of skills around team management and hiring unless you move into more of an enterprise model.

So how does freelance marketing stack up against some of the other business models that are out there? In short, other common and popular business models are much riskier. It's important to understand the risks so you can take a strategic approach to choosing the model that's right for you.

Dropshipping

Dropshipping is a fairly recent business model that became popular over the last three to five years. Rather than owning a product, you promote physical products to potential customers even though you don't manufacture or have that product in inventory anywhere. You're selling something that you don't own.

Let's say someone orders a product from your website. You then buy that exact product at a lesser cost on discount websites like Walmart.com or Alibaba.com and then have those websites ship the item directly to the end consumer. You pocket the difference.

One of the biggest challenges of this business model is that you create a poor customer experience. Although your customer buys the product from your website, when their product shows up on their doorstep a few days (or several weeks) later, the box is branded with Walmart or an unknown Chinese label instead of your branding.

You're also building no real enterprise value for your business at all. Your whole business is basically smoke and mirrors. In freelance marketing, however, you build real assets that you can sell—namely, your email list and sales funnels. I have friends who have done this; I also sold an email list and a sales funnel in 2019.

Probably the biggest threat that you face as a dropshipper is that you cannot advertise. As online businesses, we need to be able to advertise in order to generate customers to buy our products and services. But Facebook, YouTube, Google, Yahoo, Bing, Instagram, and Twitter and every other major platform out there have banned dropshippers from advertising. Once they flag you as a dropshipper, they ban your ad accounts completely.

Why? Because they want to protect their user experience, and you create a poor user experience when you sell under one store name, but your customer receives a package branded with another (often unknown) store name. You especially hurt the customer experience when you sell something that ships from China, which usually takes four to six weeks to get to the customer. All the major players want those types of businesses off their platforms.

Can you make money with dropshipping? Yes. Will it be around in the next three to five years? Doubtful.

By the way, dropshippers sell physical products, so the margins are really tight. Once you factor in the cost of ads, the product itself, and the cost of shipping, you're doing a lot of work to make maybe $10 per every $150 worth of product that you sell. On top of that, you have the headache of tracking all your purchases and dealing with angry clients and negative reviews when things don't show up (or take forever to arrive). That does not sound fun to me.

Amazon

Selling on Amazon is similar to dropshipping in that you are selling physical goods delivered by a third party, Amazon, to the consumer. The difference is that you have to own the inventory (and prove it to Amazon) or send it to Amazon for fulfillment. That's called FBA, or Fulfilled By Amazon, and it's the most common form of an Amazon business.

As an Amazon FBA business, you don't have to handle shipping, returns, or stocking inventory. But you've still got to put the money upfront to acquire the inventory for your business. That means doing a substantial amount of research to figure out what products are selling on the platform and then finding a manufacturer that can create a comparable product for you and put your label on it.

Thus, there are no differentiators in the marketplace with Amazon, meaning there are very few sellers on Amazon that truly have a unique product. When you go do a search on Amazon, you'll often see listings from multiple sellers with the same product picture but different brand packaging. That's because they're all selling the same thing. They may each list under a different brand name but most of it's coming from the same manufacturer.

The end result is that sellers end up competing solely based on price, not value. I call this a *Vicious* Business Model. But instead, you want to base your business on a *Virtuous* Business Model.

The **Vicious Business Model** is a race to the bottom. Say a certain item sells for $100, and you want to enter the market for that product, so you have to find a way to sell it for $90. Somebody else enters the same market, so they find a way to sell it for $80, then $70, then $60. Before you know it, you're trying to give the damn thing away for free.

When you keep trying to make a product cheaper so you can compete on price, what happens to the value? It diminishes. Why? Because you can't create the same product for a lower price without taking some shortcuts. When the product quality goes down, the customer experience does too, and your ability to succeed as a business decreases because you're making smaller and smaller margins. You have less ability to compete for customer acquisition because you're making less money for each sale.

In the **Virtuous Business Model,** you compete based on value, not price. You say, "Hey if that company is selling the product or service for $100, what could I add to be able to sell it for $1,000?"

And then somebody else looks at you selling it for $1,000 and goes, "Wow! They're selling that for $1,000? What additional value could I add? How else could I serve the customer to justify a price tag of $10,000?"

What happens is the product quality gets better, the customer experience gets better, and the business that's willing to innovate and add value to the product or service has an ever-increasing likelihood of success because the margins on their per unit sale continue to increase.

So not only is it better to compete based on value, it's more virtuous—in other words, more ethical. You don't have that ability on Amazon.

Another problem with an Amazon store is that you have to be careful what product class you get into because you may find yourself up against too big of a competitor. One of the strategies that big Amazon sellers use is to sell their products at a loss long enough to squeeze smaller folks out of the market. If they've got deeper pockets and have been on the platform long enough, they will just keep cutting down their product price, and will even sell at a loss to eliminate direct competitors.

Amazon even competes with its own sellers on the platform. Amazon owns hundreds, maybe thousands of brands that are sold on the platform, because when they see a product doing well, they will go and develop that product themselves. Obviously, no seller on the platform has pockets deeper than a trillion-dollar company that owns both the platform and the product. Amazon is slowly squeezing businesses right off the platform.

By the way, I tried starting an Amazon business. A few years ago, we identified Hydro Flask as a product that we wanted to compete with. We found a manufacturer in China, and our initial upfront estimate for the product alone was going to be about $5,000 to buy the number of units we needed to qualify to list as an Amazon store. When I did a side-by-side comparison of how much money I would make by investing $5,000 into my freelance marketing business versus launching an Amazon business, here's what I found.

Conservatively, I could get a three-to-one return on my freelance marketing business. So my $5,000 would bring in $15,000. On Amazon, when all was said and done, I might make $7,000 on that $5,000 investment, and have to do a lot more work for that small margin. Eventually, I decided not to launch an Amazon store.

Buying inventory also has risk attached because you have no guarantee you'll be able to sell it all. A close buddy of mine also tried to launch an Amazon store. After spending $5,000 on inventory, his product was rejected by Amazon. He was stuck with $5,000 of inventory sitting in his garage with no way to sell it. The worst part was that he was rejected simply because he missed something in the fine print about warning labels that had to be on the product. Instead, he went the freelance marketing route and has now made over $3 million executing what I've taught him.

Another problem with Amazon is its high fees. They take a significant portion of the revenue and also charge a substantial fee for managing the inventory and the shipping. Realistically, you're looking at maybe

10% margins on a lot of products—up to 25% if you're lucky. That means that you have to sell a million dollars worth of products to clear six figures. Plus you have to outlay the cash upfront. You do have some initial costs with freelance marketing if you're paying for advertising, but it's nothing close to the amount of money you'd have to spend upfront to sell a million dollars worth of products on Amazon.

Real Estate Investing

I once spent two years selling a real estate investment education product with the intention of eventually building an investment portfolio, and my consensus is that this is a tough business model for a beginner. I'm not saying that it's impossible to be successful in this business model, I'm just saying it's a lot harder, in my experience. Here's why.

There are lots of folks out there touting real estate deals with zero money out of pocket. What they don't tell you is that those deals are few and far between. In fact, there's only one strategy that I know of that truly requires zero money out of pocket—or at least there's no money out of *your* pocket. Instead, you have to find somebody else who's willing to put up the funds and trusts your ability to manage their investment.

A lot of the marketing around real estate investment is misleading because either you have good money, good credit, or good relationships with people who have money or good credit. If you don't have at least one of those things, you're shit out of luck.

There's also significant risk involved once you start putting cash into a deal. With real estate, we're talking huge amounts of money, too. Most deals require tens of thousands of dollars upfront. If you don't have the money, you can borrow it, but you must have a credit score of at least 720 to 740, depending on the lender. If you don't have that, then you need to have people in your network who are willing to invest tens of thousands of dollars upfront in order to help you with a deal.

I know several people who are successful in real estate, but they all started out with either great credit, a wad of cash to invest, or friends/family who helped them get a jump start. If you don't have one of those three things going for you, I wouldn't even consider this business model.

With the way the real estate market is today, it's harder and harder to get into investing and manage it successfully. Any business in any industry is subject to market shifts, but in real estate, those fluctuations are drastic and quick. Yes, there are real estate investors who can succeed in any market. If you have great capital and great credit, and you have the ability to sustain during market shifts, you can adapt your model and succeed. But it's risky for a total beginner.

You also have to have excellent sales skills. You have to sell the property owner on doing a deal with you, or you have to sell the bank on funding the deal. You may also have to sell the potential investor on investing in your deal. And your sales skills have to be much more honed to be able to pull off deals worth hundreds of thousands, or even millions, of dollars.

One of the things I love about freelance marketing is that you don't have to be a great salesperson. Most people don't like selling. So if that's you, and you don't have the three resources I mentioned, I would say real estate investing is a no-go.

Airbnb

This model is similar to real estate investing, except that you're either buying properties to list as a vacation rental on a platform like Airbnb or Vrbo, or you're leasing properties from an owner to sublet.

If you buy a property to operate as an Airbnb, you obviously have all the same risks as investing in real estate. If you sublease a property instead in order to earn vacation rental income, you are subject to the terms of that lease with that owner. This means if you have no renters in that property for an extended period of time, you're still responsible for paying the lease. And if you are unable to pay the lease, the owner can take you to court and force you to pay. You could even end up having your income garnished to pay off the lease.

Airbnb is also risky because municipalities around the world keep changing their laws around short-term rentals. The best place to have an Airbnb is in a location that a lot of people want to travel to. But your most profitable markets are highly inclined to change the Airbnb laws in order to support renters if there's a housing shortage in that area, or to support local businesses—especially hotels, casinos, and others in the hospitality industry. Airbnb has cost that industry billions of dollars, and many towns and cities are pushing back. So, you run the risk of buying a property and then losing the ability to earn vacation rental income from it.

I've seen this happen to friends. One of the previous videographers on my media team—a smart dude, by the way—started buying real estate in the financial crash of 2008. He once owned eight properties in Las Vegas that did well in the vacation rental market until the city changed its Airbnb laws. Suddenly, six of his properties were no longer eligible to be on the platform, and he was forced to sell. Luckily for him, he had held onto those long enough that he had equity, and he was able to get out from under those properties without damaging his financial picture.

That's not the case for a lot of people. An Airbnb business can go under overnight due to powers outside of your control. In Hawaii, the rules have changed so many times it's impossible for many owners to stay abreast of the laws. I've seen this happen to friends who were eventually forced to sell because they were losing so much money on their properties.

Airbnb businesses are subject to a lot of variables outside of your control. I tend to think that total beginners should stay away from things this risky.

Cryptocurrency Investing

Before we talk about cryptocurrency investing, let's first let's talk about what investing is. Investing is buying something that is valuable—something that you think will have a future value greater than what you pay now. Essentially, you buy below what you hope the future value will be.

I'll be completely upfront and say that buying cryptocurrency isn't investing at all—it's 100 percent high-stakes gambling. Sure, cryptocurrency is popular—you'll hear about plenty of people who went from zero dollars to multimillionaires, but what you don't hear about are the tens of thousands of dead bodies left behind in their wake.

The vast majority of people have not experienced any real success. Bitcoin has not kept a single one of the promises made in the theoretical problems it was supposed to solve. It's like zero for 100. Don't get me wrong, I have cryptocurrency—a few hundred thousand dollars worth of it. But I'm also aware that I am using that money as high stakes gambling, not as an investment. And while that might sound like a lot of money to some folks, it's a small fraction of my net worth, so I can afford the risk. That's like someone with $100 in their pocket betting a penny—they're not going to feel it. But unfortunately, that's not what most people are doing.

I tend to see Cryptocurrencies, NFTs, and any of these other new, exciting, popular opportunities that take social media by storm as a major red flag. I used to think it was smart to get in on something early. Now that I'm wise, I realize that it's foolish, and rarely, if ever, do I want to be an early adopter of anything.

I am, however, a massive fan of investing and a strong proponent of it. I have a whole team that manages an investment portfolio for me. If you read any book on long-term wealth, it is always going to include some form of investing. I'm all for buying great companies at great prices and holding onto those companies as they increase in value for several decades.

See, the "secret" to wealth is no secret at all: simply earn more than you spend. Save the rest and invest it. That's the whole game.

With that said, I'm guessing that you didn't exactly get your hands on this book to learn how to get rich over the next forty to fifty years, right? I strongly encourage you to invest, but if you're looking to quit your job in the next three to five years, investing isn't going to do that for you. Freelance marketing is.

Freelance Marketing

Now let's see how freelance marketing lines up against all the strategies we've discussed. First off, it requires zero cost out of pocket for a product or service to sell. That means zero product development cost, zero cost of inventory, and zero product research. Instead, you rely on other businesses to do all that stuff for you.

Next, your initial startup overhead is slim. We're talking less than $200 per month in overhead for some basic tools, like a website builder and an email marketing platform (we'll cover all the tools you need in the next chapter). How many business models exist in the world that allow you to start a business from scratch for less than $200 a month? Not many. You also start out with the massive advantage of knowing whether or not the product or service that you're going to sell is *sellable*. Because with a little bit of research, you can figure out how well a product or service is selling (we'll talk more about that in Chapter 3).

The only real cost or upfront risk in freelance marketing is your advertising cost, which can be avoided altogether if you choose organic or social media strategies to grow your business. Here's an example. At the time of writing this book, I have a client who started working with us seven months ago. Three months ago, she opened a TikTok account, and by her second month on the platform, she generated over $41,000 in commissions, with $0 out of pocket, promoting one of the products we recommend inside Fullstaq Marketer. You can learn more about how to launch your business with our Fullstaq products by visiting iiexplained.com.

I do recommend paid advertising, even in the beginning, because it's a much more scalable strategy (we'll dive deeper into scalability later in the book), but it's the only financial risk involved. And at the same time, you get to fix that cost based on whatever your risk tolerance is. Some of our clients will start with as little as five to ten dollars a day in ad spend. So they cut out a cup or two of coffee a day and that's their entire risk. There's no massive loan to invest thousands (or hundreds of thousands) of dollars upfront. There's no putting inventory on credit cards. You're able to minimize and control the risk and stay within a threshold that's comfortable and safe for you.

I'm pretty risk averse, and I'm not a big fan of seeing others take on massive risk either. Because you don't have inventory or any substantial overhead, market shifts make little difference to you as a freelance marketer. If a competitor comes out with a product that devalues the product or service that you're currently selling, that's not a major risk because you have no overhead—you can find another great product or service to offer instead. If rules change on the advertising platforms so that you can no longer advertise your product or service, again, there's no risk to you because you have no overhead. And as a freelance marketer, you learn to adapt quickly to market changes anyway.

People think that when there's a recession or depression that money stops moving. But money never stops moving—it just shifts to move in different directions. And if you're a freelance marketer and really understand the power of advertising, you're going to make money regardless of what the market is doing because you'll always be able to put yourself in front of the money, no matter where it's headed.

Let's get started.

Chapter 3

Getting Started

In order to start your own freelance marketing business you need three things:

1. **An Offer:** A product or a service that solves a real problem in the marketplace.
2. **An Audience:** The group of people that has a problem that is solved by the offer you promote.
3. **A Sales Funnel:** The automated system to handle sales of the product or service that you will promote.

When looking for an offer, I stay inside of what we call **The Big Three**—or the mega niches. Those are **money and finance, love and relationships, and health and wellness**. We joke that everybody wants to get laid, get paid, and live forever. The basic principle is that the larger the audience or the larger the problem that you're solving in the marketplace, the more scalable your income will be—and this is true for any business, not just freelance marketers. The mega niches have the biggest audiences and encompass the majority of the offers that are out there in the marketplace.

Any one of those niches also includes a wide array of business opportunities. In money and finance, for example, you could focus on stock market investing, real estate investing, options trading, and so on.

Inside of love and relationships, you could focus on dating tips or how to repair a marriage. One market in this field that really took off in the early 2000s was teaching men how to become "pickup artists." There are also offers that teach people how to win their ex back—these are all really common. And then when it comes to health and wellness, you can focus on weight loss, muscle gain for men, hair loss products, protein shakes, workout programs, or hypnosis programs that help people stop eating, etc.

If you find a really niche problem, there is a trade-off. On the one hand, it's easier for you to generate sales revenue. For example, if I want to promote a product or service that helps dentists find new clients, I can use precise language that only dentists understand, speaking to them in terms that quickly build their trust in me. It's easier to stand out in that sub-niche because the market is small, which makes conversions (sales) simpler. The tradeoff is that income is also going to be pretty small compared to larger niches.

I would rather go broad with bigger, more scalable audiences because I have all the skills necessary for me to compete in a bigger market. And those are the skills that make you millions of dollars.

Yes, if you choose a broad audience there's going to be much more competition in your marketplace. It'll be more challenging for you to build trust between your prospect and your brand or offer. But ultimately, your efforts will be more rewarding because once you crack that market, it'll be easier to scale to five figures a month, and then multi-five figures or even six figures a month because there's a much bigger audience to sell to. If I'm going to work just as hard to make a little bit of money versus a lot of money, why wouldn't I just make a lot of money?

The Ultimate Hack: Find an Offer and Audience That Inspire You

As a new freelance marketer, I got into the money-making space because I loved learning about how to make money. It was easy for me to wake up each morning and read books, do research, listen to podcasts, watch YouTube videos, and learn what I could about how to make money because I found the topic so inspiring. It was easy for me to email my list consistently and write compelling advertisements. Nobody had to drag me out of bed every day; I just loved running my business.

I have a friend named Paul who sells offers in the barbecue niche. But the thing is, he *hates* barbecuing. He has nothing in common with his ideal customer or any interest in the niche. And the result is that he's never been able to get that business to make more than a little over six figures per year in profit, even though he's sold millions of dollars of product in that industry. Imagine how successful he'd be if he devoted all that time, energy, and expertise to a niche he loved!

I know a lot of people like Paul who have made money building businesses around which they have no inspiration, and at the end of the day, they're miserable. I would rather spend my time building a business that's going to fill my soul than a business that's only going to fill my bank account.

When you're thinking about starting a freelance marketing business, consider the things you're already interested in. What do you love doing in your free time? What are your favorite hobbies? What would you love to learn about that you haven't had time to dive into as deeply as you'd like? Start here to narrow down your ideal market.

On-Market Offers vs. Off-Market Offers

Now let's look at where to find offers to sell to your chosen audience. There are plenty of ways to find offers, but the easiest and most seamless way is through affiliate networks, which are platforms that connect product owners with freelance marketers. Offers found through affiliate networks are called **on-market** offers. Say a product owner has something great to offer but no idea how to sell or promote it. And a freelance marketer has a lot of skill around selling and promoting, but no product. Affiliate networks provide a platform where product owners and freelance marketers can find each other.

Two of the biggest affiliate networks in the industry are ClickBank and Digistore24. Typically, these platforms allow you to sort through offers based on niches and sub-niches. And more importantly, you can sort the offers in a particular niche based on the earning potential of each offer.

Let's say you want to start with something that's going to make the most money. Remember, you're going to do the same amount of work whether the offer sells well or not, so you may as well pick the most profitable, right? Weight loss is a great niche, so say you open ClickBank and search "weight loss." You can then sort the offers by the highest earnings per sale.

The next thing to consider for each offer is what ClickBank calls the "Gravity Score." ClickBank is vague about how they assign this score, but essentially it is a performance metric that tells you how many units of a particular product have sold recently. The Gravity Score tells you whether or not that product is moving right now on the market and whether people are having success promoting it. If you can find an offer in a niche that you're interested in and inspired about, and it's in the top 5% of offers on the platform in terms of what it pays per sale, *and* it's in the top 5% in terms of how much volume is currently moving, then you've probably got a winning offer.

Through my company, Fullstaq Marketer, our clients are able to sell the exact same products that we've already earned over $100 million selling. We make it easy for our clients to know that they are selling a product that converts because we've already done it. We also give our freelance marketing clients all of the additional materials necessary in order to promote those products successfully. That includes websites, landing pages, email copy—we even show them where we're running ads so that they can get their products in front of the same people that we're getting our products in front of—an audience that has already brought us $100 million in revenue. We give our freelance marketers a shortcut between their learning curve and seeing results.

We aren't the only company in the world to do this, but it's certainly not common. As a much more niched version of an affiliate network, our real advantage is that we take care of our customers more than anybody else in our space. Again, you can get access to these products too. Simply visit iiexplained.com to learn how to get started.

Another place to find offers is to approach product owners directly to ask if they are open to you promoting their offer as an affiliate. These are called **off-network** offers. Some product owners will only manage affiliates through their own in-house teams. A good example of an off-market offer might be the products and services sold by Tony Robbins; the last time I checked, he didn't have an offer listed on the networks, but works with freelance markers via their own affiliate programs. In order to become an affiliate of his offers, I would go to his company website, fill out a form to be approved as an affiliate, and then I would be able to promote his company's products.

When I first started my coaching business, our first affiliate approached us in exactly this way. We didn't have an affiliate program at the time, or even the resources to support one. But when this guy reached out to me directly, he said that he had watched my presentation, bought the program, and had started going through the course material.

"This is phenomenal stuff!" he told me. "I'd love to promote your offer."

I got on a call with him to find out whether the idea was even worth my time. It turned out that he had an email list of 100,000 people, which told me right away that he was definitely a player in the industry. The long and the short of it was that we built a sales funnel unique to him, along with a whole new affiliate tracking system.

Within six months, he was sending us $1 million in revenue per month by himself, and he was earning a few million dollars a year *on our product alone*. Ours was the first product through which he'd ever made a million dollars-plus in affiliate earnings in a single year. He was already good at what he did, but he'd never had an offer that converted as well as ours did.

The point is, never underestimate the value of approaching people directly and finding a way to become their affiliate. The advantage here is that you have no competition in the marketplace, and you can negotiate the terms of the agreement. Typically, an off-market product owner will be a bit more flexible because they're not working with a ton of other affiliates, and they're not beholden to the rules on the different networks. Off-market deals take a lot more time to chase down, but they can be more lucrative.

By the way, you don't have to accept affiliate terms for offers that you find through networks like ClickBank and Digistore. You can always negotiate terms upfront. This is important because many freelance marketers don't realize this. Each offer will have published terms that include your commissions, how often you get paid out, etc. But you can negotiate those terms upfront.

Even when I was on a brand new platform I had no relationship with, I would always negotiate those terms. I'd say, "Hey, I have a list that's X size. I run X per day in ads, and I'm wondering if you guys would be willing to pay me X?" Sometimes, I'd also find the same offer on a different network, and I'd compare the two and use any differences to negotiate better terms.

Negotiating better terms get easier once you have some success under your belt. If you're a freelance marketer who's already built a sizable email list and you've proven your marketing chops (i.e. you've made your first six figures or so), then these networks will fight over keeping you. As a freelance marketer myself, I can tell you that every time there is an event in our industry, networks reach out to ask if I'm going to be there. They have bought me dinners, fine bottles of wine, and great cigars all as an attempt to court me into working with their networks exclusively. They've even offered me dedicated teams and representatives—the ultra VIP experience.

If you make yourself invaluable in the marketplace, both networks and individual companies will work hard to get your business.

The Sales Funnel: Your "Money Machine"

Now that you've identified a niche you want to be in that inspires you, and an offer you want to promote, you'll need to set up your sales funnel. This step is the least straightforward and takes the most amount of skill and time to learn, which is why I've devoted all of Chapter 5 to discussing sales funnels in even more detail. But you start by figuring out where your ideal audience hangs out online. What social networks are they on? What websites do they visit most often? What books do they read? What authors do they follow? What television news stations do they watch? What about online newsletters—which ones do they subscribe to? Once you do figure out where your audience is, you'll need to build a sales funnel to help you get in front of that audience.

What is a sales funnel? Well, imagine you have a machine that sits on your nightstand. Each night you go to bed and whatever money you put in the machine, when you wake up the next morning, you have five times that amount of money waiting for you. That night, you put more money into the machine. The next morning, you have five times that amount of money again.

If you had a money machine like this, how much money would you put into it? Probably every penny you owned, right? I don't know about you, but I'd be going down the street, knocking on all my neighbor's doors, trying to get them to give me money, offering them a three-to-one return while I kept the rest for myself!

A sales funnel is that money machine. Specifically, it's an automated online system that does your marketing, selling, telling and explaining for you to your prospects, and it allows you to run 85% to 90% of your business on autopilot.

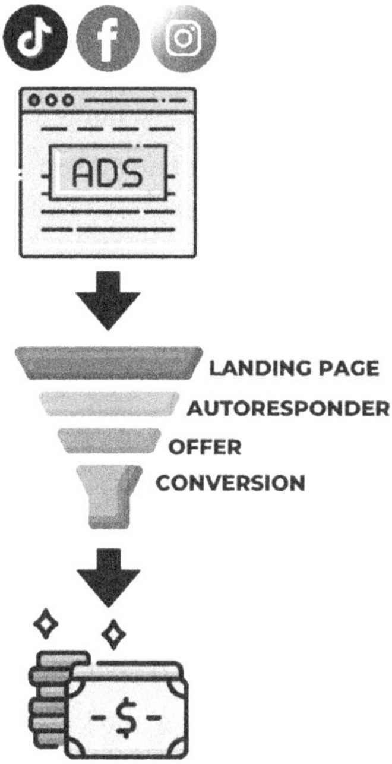

Say you've identified the products and services you want to offer and have chosen an ideal audience to market to. But rather than send people directly to your offer, you create a landing page—basically a simplified version of a website—that presells the offer. Let's say you're selling fat-burning soup recipes for weight loss (for the record, this is a real offer available on several networks). When people buy the program, they get a set of recipes and directions to replace at least one meal a day with these soups. Imagine hitting a web page that says...

The Fat Burning Secrets Doctors Don't Want You to Know...

How to Melt Fat Fast Without Starving Yourself, Counting Calories, Or Ever Breaking A Sweat!

Enter your email below for more information

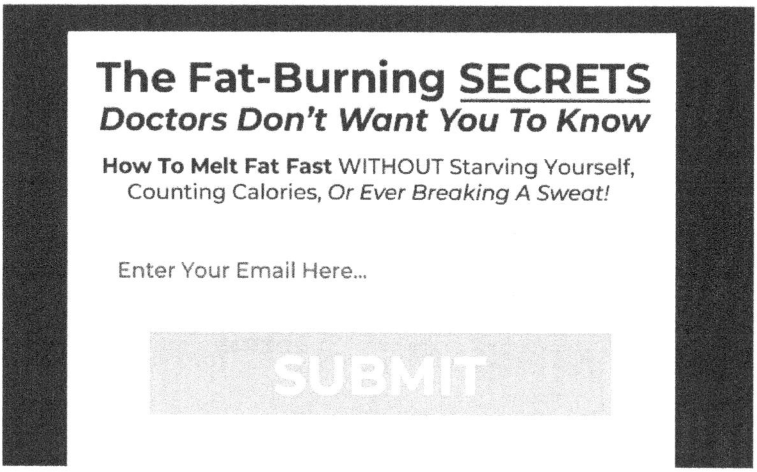

Do you think that if someone who is serious about losing weight hits that page they might hand over their email address to get more information? You bet your @$$ they would!

Now you need to drive traffic to that landing page through advertisements on platforms where your audience hangs out. This time, you need to reverse engineer the copy based on what your ideal audience is interested in so that you can attract their attention.

Let's say your ideal audience mostly hangs out on Facebook. Based on your research, you know that the people most likely to buy your offer are predominantly women interested in things like CrossFit, weight loss, and healthy dieting. Your Facebook ad might say something like:

Hey, Ladies! Want to get your beach body back before summer? Did you know there's a secret set of fat-burning recipes doctors hope you never find out about? Click here to learn more.

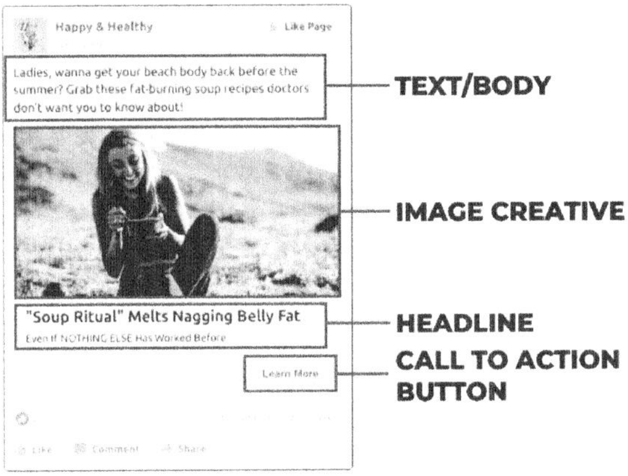

Do you see how the ad preframes what they'll see on the landing page, which in turn, preframes what they'll see on the offer page? That's basically how you sandwich the funnel between the offer and the audience.

Once people hit your landing page, you promise a potential solution in exchange for their contact information. You can ask for any information you want, but obviously, the more information you ask for, the less likely it is that someone will hand it over. So you want to ask for the least amount of information necessary for you to generate a sale. Typically a landing page will only ask for an email address, or name and email. The greater the offer on the other end of that page, the more information you can ask for.

Using the example from Figure 3.1, all you're offering is a free video, so you're not going to ask for much more than an email address. But let's say you're offering a full six-module course with fourteen lessons to walk people through the process of melting fat without starving themselves or breaking a sweat. Now you can ask for a name, email address, and even phone number. Some people would even sell that product right from the landing page and ask for a credit card.

Typically though, at this stage, you are just beginning a relationship with prospects, so you want to earn their trust (and their business) by giving something away that will help solve a part of their problem. Once someone signs up via your landing page, their information goes into a database called an autoresponder.

The Fortune Is in The Follow-Up

Most people don't buy the first time they see your offer—they need time to consider, and some convincing that it's right for them. Your sales funnel allows you to automate this process for every single prospect in a "set it and forget it" system using a tool called an autoresponder. The autoresponder allows you to follow up on autopilot via a series of pre-written emails sent automatically to each prospect on a schedule you set up ahead of time. These follow-up emails help convert as many prospects as possible into customers.

The follow-up sequence includes three types of emails:

1. Social Proof
2. Risk-Reversal
3. Bonuses

Social proof includes testimonials the company has received praising the product, or snippets of comments from social sites that prove that your product has worked for other people in similar situations to your prospect. Social proof is powerful because it helps your prospects trust that your offer will give them the results they are paying for.

Your emails also need to overcome your prospects' objections, the most common being, "I don't have time!" and "I don't have money." This is why we include risk reversal emails in our follow up. This email helps people see that the price of *not* buying the product is greater than the price of buying it. For example, let's take a look at our weight loss offer. When it comes to weight, the prospect likely already knows that obesity is tied closely to a shorter lifespan. If someone is overweight, they're more likely to develop health problems that might cause them to die sooner. So your risk-reversal emails might talk about the price your prospect could pay if they *don't* buy these weight loss recipes.

In regards to the money objection, an email might say something like, "Can you really afford not to do this? Would you rather pay the price of getting your hands on these recipes… or pay the expensive medical bills that come along with not paying attention to your health sooner? Which do you think costs more?" You want your prospect to see that the price of missing out is greater than the price of buying.

To address the time objection we might say something like, "Which do you think costs more time? A few minutes per day prepping a scrumptious soup… or dying years earlier than you had to because you weren't willing to invest in your health? "

As you can see, these emails aren't polite. They're polarizing. That's intentional. We're not here to make friends. We're here to make sales. You'll go broke trying to please people so don't fall into that trap.

The third type of email in our sequence includes information about bonuses that add more value to the offer and enhancements the prospect can't get anywhere else. We'll talk more about bonuses in Chapter 9, where you'll learn how to create those extra benefits that make the offers you're promoting irresistible.

In Chapter 7 on copywriting, you'll learn more about how to write effective email sequences that convert, and Chapter 10 covers email management in greater detail. But for now, it's important to understand that you will pre-write a series of emails that contain social proof, overcome objections, and offer exclusive bonuses—and schedule those emails to be sent by your autoresponder automatically whenever someone hands you their email on your landing page. Write these emails once, and they will sell your offers 24-7 without any extra effort from you.

You can set up your autoresponder according to any schedule you choose. When I was a freelancer, at one point I compiled a 90-day email sequence, which meant that when somebody opted into my list, they would get 90 days of follow-up emails automatically. This is how I was able to take extended vacations and still earn money. I could be sitting at the beach, hanging out with friends, watching movies, or out to dinner, and my automated system would continue to put my offers in front of my audience, making sales without any additional effort from me.

The Power of Leverage

Archimedes once said, "Give me a lever long enough, and a fulcrum on which to place it, and I shall move the world." Let's take a moment to understand the amount of leverage you have with freelance marketing versus all of the other opportunities we talked about prior.

Say that you've written one good email that converts 1% of readers into a buyer. Now you've set up that email to go out automatically to every potential lead that I generate. If you have 1,000 leads in your pipeline, that one email gets sent to 1,000 people, automatically converting into ten sales. With 10,000 leads in your pipeline, that one email is sent 10,000 times, resulting in 100 sales. If you have just one piece of great sales material, you do the work once and leverage the benefit over and over again. All you have to do to increase sales is get that one email in front of more people.

This is how you decouple time and money. You're not likely to find this much leverage in any other opportunity out there.

Remember, in a freelance marketing business, you don't have to also make the product. Other businesses have to make the products, then keep churning out content to lead people to a website, and then deliver the products or services they sell. But with the freelance model, once you have a great offer and sales funnel, all you have to do each day is just manage your advertisements.

People have a hard time believing it, but at one point, I was making $30,000 to $40,000 per month literally working two hours a day. I understand why it's hard to comprehend that because most people don't have the kind of leverage a freelance marketer has. Most people have to put in more hours to make more dollars. But once I set up my sales funnel, if I wanted to make more money, all I had to do was increase my advertising dollars. That meant I generated more leads daily, which meant more people going through the sales funnel, which meant more people buying on the other end.

Eventually, my time and earnings decoupled. Literally, my days would look like this: I'd wake up, make my coffee and relax over breakfast. Sometimes I'd walk down to the beach and jump in the ocean for a swim. Afterward, I'd check in to see how my ads were performing, cutting ones that weren't doing well, and slowly scaling up ad spend on ones that continued to perform. On some days, I might write a broadcast email to my list, but that was it.

That was my whole work day, and I helped dozens of other people get there even before I launched Fullstaq Marketer. This is what's possible for you too.

In the next chapter, I'll show you the best products to sell right out of the gate. These products will make you millions, and all you have to do is follow the step-by-step guide right here in this book.

Chapter 4

Million Dollar Offers

High quality products create high quality results and therefore demand high quality prices. As freelance marketers, not only is it better for our business to sell high quality, high priced products but, as you're about to see, it's the most virtuous way to conduct business. Period.

In Chapter 3, we talked about the difference between selling to a niche audience or going broad to reach more people. So should you sell a high priced product few can afford or a low priced product just about anyone can afford? Let's compare the two options.

Say you have two freelance marketers, Person A and Person B. They're both selling in the same niche, solving the same problem, for the same people. Person A is selling a $200 product that pays them $100 commission every time they make a sale. Even on a fixed income, most people can find a way to afford this product. Person B is selling a $10,000 product that pays a $4,000 commission whenever they make a sale.

Which person do you think is more likely to win?

Every time I ask this question in our Business Launch Challenge we get answers that are close to a 60/40 split, where the majority of people think that the cheaper product is the better product to sell. Let me break down exactly why that's illogical and doesn't work.

The $10,000 product pays 40 times more commission ($4,000) than the $200 product ($100 commission), right? The common myth is that a product that costs more money will be harder to sell. But let's think about that for a moment.

Is it really 40 times harder to sell the $10,000 product than the $200 product? Do you think the person who's selling a $10,000 product has to run 40 times as many ads? Do they have to write 40 times as many emails, generate 40 times as many leads, overcome 40 times as many objections, and talk to 40 times as many skeptical spouses? No. True, it *is* harder to sell a higher-priced product, but it's not *proportionately* harder.

Let me illustrate my point with a couple of examples you can probably relate to. In real estate, it's just as easy to sell a million-dollar home as it is to sell a $300,000 home. Actually, it's easier, because the million-dollar buyer already has their down payment set up, and most likely a good credit score. They're a little bit more sophisticated in how they've managed their money so they know what they can afford and have all their ducks in a row.

In 2020/2021, when the market was exploding here in Las Vegas, people were moving in from California, buying multi-million-dollar homes sight unseen. The selling realtor didn't have to walk their clients through fifty homes to sell that one multi-million-dollar house. The buyers were so eager to leave California for whatever reason (probably taxes) that they just bought without stepping foot inside the house. If I were in real estate today, I wouldn't waste my time selling $300,000 houses because I know that I'm going to have the same number of conversations, and do the same amount of paperwork and negotiating as I would selling $3,000,000 homes. And I'd get paid way more money if I sold a $3,000,000 house over a $300,000 house.

With a higher-end product, you're selling to a different type of customer.

When I served tables in restaurants, I always wanted to work in fine dining. I could sell a bottle of wine worth $1,000 versus $100. Do you think that I had to work harder to sell a $1,000 bottle of wine? No. It took the same amount of energy to ask and answer the same questions about the customer's preferences. In fact, in most cases, I spent less energy to make more money working in fine dining.

Why? Because I had fewer tables than when I worked at a less upscale restaurant, and each person (on average) at each table spent more money, which means that I earned a bigger tip. Now, obviously, I had to be a bit more sophisticated in my skills and approach. When I worked in bars and grills I could wear shorts and a t-shirt with an apron and tennis shoes and get away with that. I could be nonchalant, and say things like, "How's it going, folks?" In fine dining, I was more formal in the way I dressed and how I spoke to my customers. The skills were a little different, but the work wasn't harder.

In the same way, it's not proportionately more difficult to sell a $200 product than a $10,000 product. So if you make more money selling something, even if it costs more, it's not proportionately more difficult to sell. Ultimately, you get a better rate of return on the time, energy and money invested in trying to make that sale. If you're going to invest time, energy and money anyway, why not get a better rate of return?

Now, not only is selling high ticket products going to pay you more, it's also more virtuous. Let me explain.

If it were true that the best way to succeed in business was to sell the cheapest product, then the aim would be to constantly under price the competition. If they're selling the same product you are for $100, you'd better find a way to sell it for $90. When they see you selling for $90, they're trying to find a way to sell it for $80. Now you're trying to find a way to sell it for $70. On and one this charade goes until you're practically giving your product away.

Now, think about this for a moment. Do you think the product quality increases when you compete on price? And what about the customer satisfaction? It doesn't take a genius to figure out that both product quality and customer satisfaction take a nosedive with this kind of thinking. That's why I call it the Vicious Pricing Model.

In contrast, let's consider the opposite for a second. You see your competitor selling a product or service for $100 and think to yourself, "Gee, with a little extra value added, I could sell that for $1,000." Next thing you know, your competitor is saying, "Shoot. They're charging

$1,000! What if I made a few tweaks and created a $10,000 option for my customers?"

Do you see where this is going? When you compete in this way, does the product or service go up or down in value? And what about the customer satisfaction? The answer is obvious. When we compete based on *value*, not *price*, we create better products and serve our customers at a higher level. That's why I call this the Virtuous Pricing Model.

Therefore, not only will you make money a whole lot faster by selling high ticket offers, but doing so is even more *virtuous*.

Can you see how Person B has a clear advantage with their $10,000 offer? Might it be a little harder to make a sale? Yes. But not *proportionately* more difficult to make a sale. Add that to the fact that it's ultimately more *virtuous* and you can rest assured that you're on the right track.

In my experience, the only reason you may tend to think that Person A might have the advantage is because if you're struggling financially, you think everyone is struggling financially. In psychology, that's called projection. Whatever you experience, you project onto the world around you.

When you're a beginner, you're going to make more mistakes in your advertisements, and those mistakes cost you money. Maybe your ad copy isn't as compelling, or you're awkward in your video advertisements; perhaps you're not the best at sales conversions yet.

Remember: you're learning, and this is normal. However, all these mistakes cost you a little bit of money, which means you pay more to acquire each customer. But that's okay—you will get better.

If you're a beginner and you have a high-ticket product to sell, you can afford to make more mistakes. That's why in our curriculum, we encourage all of our clients to sell a high-ticket product to start. The higher commission helps mitigate those mistakes and make profits faster.

In Part 2, you'll learn how to set up all the components of your digital sales funnel (your money machine) and how to drive traffic through advertising. This is how you bring in leads for your email list. Together, your email list and sales funnel are your most valuable assets. Once you understand how all the puzzle pieces come together, you'll learn how to maximize your earnings from this vertical selling system that you have built.

Part 2

Traffic

Chapter 5

Building Your Money Machine

As you learned in Chapter 3, a sales funnel (a.k.a. money machine) is nothing more than a well-designed buying sequence: a set of digital tools that work together to engineer a buying process. A sales funnel consists of:

1. Advertisements
2. A simple website
3. An autoresponder
4. Your offer

You are surrounded by sales funnels, but the average person doesn't use that verbiage to describe it. Here's what I mean. Your grocery store is a sales funnel. Think about it. The reason most grocery stores put the meat and produce at the back of the store is because that's what most people come to the grocery store to buy, and the store owners want you to walk past all the other tempting products on your way to get what you came for. Stores are designed to guide you on a buying journey through the liquor aisles, the candy bars you swore off, and the bags of chips you've been trying to avoid. The hope is that, on your way toward the meat and veggies, you'll load up your cart with a whole bunch of things that weren't even on your list. If grocery store tycoons built their shops according to most people's shopping lists, they'd make a lot less money. Stores are built to force you to see things you didn't intend to buy.

Movie theaters are a sales funnel too. You pay for your ticket at the front, but in order to get to your theater, you have to pass the concession stand. Inside the theater, when you're sitting waiting for your movie to play during the previews, they constantly market to you about the snacks available at the concession stand. You came to see a movie, but now you've loaded up on popcorn, candy, and soft drinks. That's a sales funnel.

IKEA is the very definition of a sales funnel. If you've ever been to an IKEA store, you know what I mean. You go in for dishware, but you've got to first walk through the living room section, the home office section, and all the kids' furniture. You follow arrows on the floor to get where you want to go, and IKEA knows exactly what route to guide you to increase its overall revenue.

A sales funnel is nothing more than a well-designed buying sequence. It's a way to push a prospect through a sales process to increase both the conversion rate (what percentage of people buy) and the "average order value" (how much they spend).

In digital sales funnels, you use a set of online tools that work together cohesively to engineer a buying process for a potential prospect. As we talked about in Chapter 3, those tools typically consist of your offer, your audience, a page builder-like tool (also referred to as a website builder or sales funnel builder), and an autoresponder.

To recap the basics you learned in Chapter 3, the sales funnel works like this:

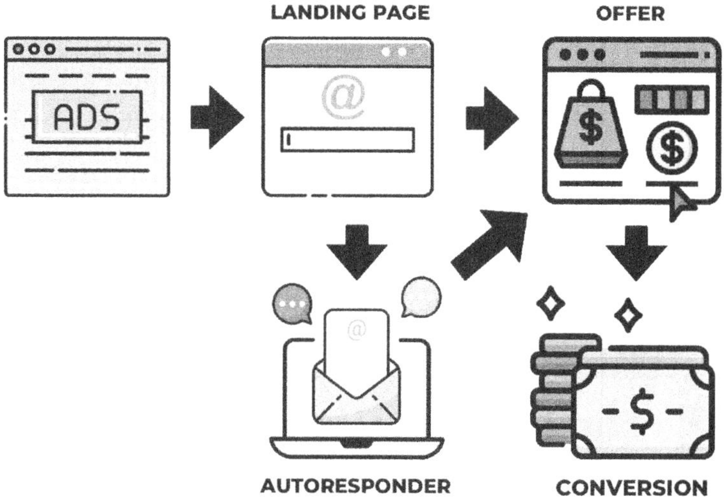

First, you place an ad online in front of your ideal prospect (we'll cover advertising in more detail in the next chapter). When our prospects see the advertisement, they click on a link and go to our simplified website—the landing page—which you create using your page builder tool. On that landing page, you write copy that pre-frames your offer. When someone is interested in that offer, they give you their contact info (usually their email address and name) in exchange for more information. Their contact information goes straight into your autoresponder, and the prospect is taken directly to the offer. The autoresponder is the email marketing tool that you use to follow up with prospects on an automated basis.

Start With The Offer, Then Reverse Engineer The Funnel

Creating your sales funnel is as simple as reverse engineering it from your offer; in fact, this is the most effective way to design your sales funnel. As an example, let's revisit the fat-burning soup recipes offer from earlier in the book. How do you introduce this offer to get the most people interested, and at the same time, only attract people who are likely to buy?

First, you need an eye-popping headline that provides a bold promise as to what someone is going to get by taking action on your page.

Next, you reverse engineer from that page to create the advertisement. To do this, you first want to identify our audience. Let's say during your research you find that the majority of buyers for this offer are female. You might target women who are interested in weight loss, healthy eating, dieting, working out, or physical fitness. You can use an image for the advertisement with a photo of a woman with the following…

Wanna get your beach body back before the summer? Check out these fat-burning soup recipes doctors don't want you to know about!

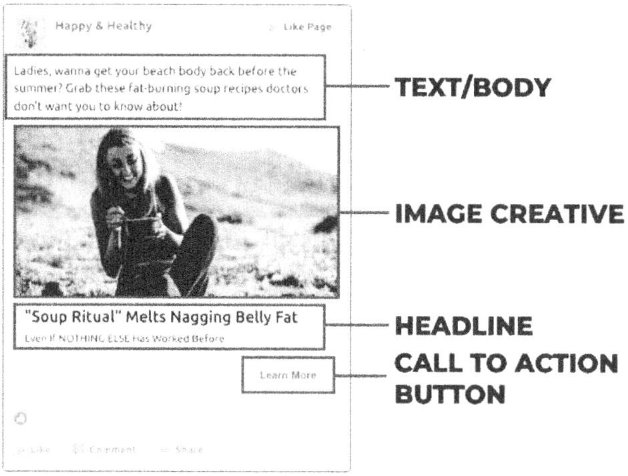

When someone clicks the link on your ad, they go straight to your landing page where they have to give you their email to access the free video that reveals the secret.

Hopefully, that video sells them on the product, but you know that the likelihood of them buying right away is pretty slim—although some do buy the first time that they see an offer. That's okay because you have their email. Through the autoresponder, you'll use email to convert your new prospect into a buyer through follow-up emails that you send automatically over time. Just like in our physical world where you walk through sales funnels at the grocery store or movie theater, your online funnel is the digital version of that same journey.

The Ascension Model vs. The Descension Model

In the world of sales funnels, there are two schools of thought: one is that you should take potential customers directly to your highest ticket offers. The idea is to decrease the amount of friction in the sales process and get as many people to see your highest ticket offer as possible. If that's not a fit, you can downsell the prospect to lower priced products or packages that fit their budget. This is the **descension model**.

Theoretically, that makes sense because the more high-ticket offers you sell, the more money you make. If people say no to your high-ticket offer, you move them to a lower-ticket offer and then steer them toward offers that decrease in price all the way to your least expensive offer.

The **ascension model** is typically what you see more often. Here, you sell an affordable product on the front end, and "upsell," or offer a series of products after the initial purchase that ascends into your highest ticket offers.

To be clear, both of these strategies work. It just depends on what audience you are marketing to, and where they fall on the scale of customer awareness. To better understand which model is best for your offer and audience so you can strategically build your sales funnel, you can use the "The Five Stages of Customer Awareness" as explained by marketing genius Eugene Schwartz in his classic book, *Breakthrough Advertising*. Every customer falls on a scale of problem awareness between one and five (where stage one is the most aware and stage five is the least). Let's use our fat-loss soup recipes example again to look at each stage.

Stage One: Problem Aware. Your prospect knows they need to get control of their health, and is on the cusp of buying from you. To get them to purchase, all you need is a strong enough offer. These customers also represent the smallest, narrowest segment of your audience.

1. **Stage Two: Problem Aware, Solution Aware.** Your prospect is already aware that you and your soup recipes can solve their problem, but they're not quite sold yet. Maybe they're just not sure how you're different from everything else in the market.
2. **Stage Three: Problem Aware, Solution Aware, But Not Aware of You.** Your prospect is looking for a solution to their problem but has no clue yet that you exist. They're already sold on the idea that special soup recipes are the solution to their problem. They just haven't found you yet.
3. **Stage Four: Problem Aware, Solution Unaware.** The prospect knows they need to do something about their health, but they're not sure what the solution is, and they've never heard of you. Should they hire a trainer? Try a Keto diet? They're not sure. You've got to convince them that your

soup recipes are the best solution, and then make your offer irresistible.

4. **Stage Five: Problem Unaware, Solution Unaware.** This person doesn't even know they have a problem, so they're not even in the market for a solution. You have to first convince them that they have a problem, then convince them there's a solution to that problem. Then, you have to convince them that your product is the best product to solve that problem. To do this, your copy needs to be strong. However, the benefit is that this audience is the biggest and broadest (i.e. the most scalable).

To summarize what this all means, the closer someone is to Stage One, the more likely they are to buy from you. The closer they are to Stage Five, the less likely they are to buy from you. Furthermore, your chances of converting someone at Stage Four, as an example, to a customer today are far *less* likely if you're using the descension model and far *more* likely if you're using the ascension model. The more money you're asking someone to invest, the more trust they need to have in you and the product you're promoting.

Another factor you want to consider when deciding whether your audience will respond better to the ascension or descension model is their sophistication. In every market, there are people who prioritize time over money and people who prioritize money over time. You've got to decide, what does your audience value more?

The more sophisticated the audience is, the better a **descension model** will work, because they typically prioritize time over money.

They would rather spend money to save time. If you are marketing to the upper echelon of market sophistication—people in Stages One to Three of customer awareness, these people are pre-sold on the type of solution you offer and want to get straight to it. They just need to know how your offer stands out from everything else they've tried.

The challenge here is that although this audience is easier to sell to, it's also much less scalable because it's the smallest. If you want a more scalable route and are willing to market to people in Stage Four or Five of customer awareness, then I suggest the **ascension model**. These people typically value money over time but represent a much bigger audience. In this case, you would promote a low-ticket front-end product and build from there.

In short, a descension funnel requires more time and energy to convert your prospect into a customer because you have to build more trust to help them justify the higher-ticket price. However, if you start with a low ticket offer (that ascends into a high-ticket offer later in the funnel) it's much easier to convert someone from a total stranger (Stages 3 through 5) into a customer.

Once a person buys a low ticket offer, they've differentiated themselves as a customer versus a lead. They have voted with their money to show you, as a business, that they are serious about solving their problem. If they've just bought a hundred dollar product, you can bet they're at least a hundred times more serious than the person who's bought nothing yet.

Next, you want to capitalize on this customer by over-delivering on the promise you made.

This is your opportunity to build trust with *your* customer. While it's true that they bought someone else's product, I like to think of them as *my* customer. When I first started as a Freelancer in 2012, I did okay. People were buying the products I was promoting but few were upgrading (which paid me even higher commissions). One day I decided to start calling the customers I was generating just to thank them for buying the product. I'd introduce myself, let them know that I wasn't with the company but just an affiliate, and offer to answer any questions they had. To my surprise, most of them started asking about the other products the company offered. By answering a few questions, customers began upgrading at rates I'd never considered possible. That meant that I earned more commissions from every customer I generated and from that day forward, I made it a point to reach out to every customer.

While it's true that it's not your *product*, this is your *business*. When possible, treat the customers you generate as if they were your own and you'll find they're even more loyal to you than the company they just purchased from.

Here's a good analogy to decide whether to employ an ascension or descension model. If you want to catch a yellowfin tuna, you can go out, bait a fishing pole, and drag it around the ocean for a few hours and hope that you end up with a few bites. Or, you can drop a big net in the water and get hundreds of fish, sift through them all and pick out only the tuna.

I prefer the latter. That's the **ascension model**.

You cast a wide net (ads), you catch lots of fish (leads on your email list), you sift through the fish (email marketing) and find the tuna (customers).

Do you have to have an email list to be a successful freelance marketer? No, but here is why it's so important to build one: The majority of people do not buy the very first time that they see an offer. Remember, the fortune is in the follow-up.

With the help of an autoresponder, your email list is basically a follow-up machine. Because of that, you could say the *real* fortune is in your email list. At Fullstaq Marketer, over 90% of the revenue we earn comes from our email follow-up sequence. One of the programs we offer is a virtual summit where we help people build their *entire* freelance marketing business from scratch and get results in just one weekend (go to iiexplained.com to sign up). During the event, we ask participants how long they've been on our email list. Like clockwork, we have folks who've been on our email list 6 months, 9 months, 18 months, 36 months and longer. In fact, at one recent event, a woman told me she'd been on our list for seven years, and this was the first time she'd bought anything! If we weren't building and nurturing an email list, we'd have left tens of millions of dollars on the table.

Not having an email list is kind of like not having a refrigerator in your house. You would literally only eat what you could kill each day, and the rest would go to waste. You need a place to incubate your potential customers until they're ready to buy. We live in an attention economy, and the person who wins is the person who can get attention, hold it, and monetize it. And the longer you hold attention, the more opportunity you have to monetize that audience. Without an email list, you're playing the game of trying to grab and monetize attention in one moment.

In the world of online business, your email list is also a real asset, worth real value. You can sell, lease, or rent your list. A few years back, I sold an email list and sales funnel. Your offers will come and go, as will your sales funnels and associated audiences. But your email list is an asset worth real value in the marketplace.

In fact, if you were to take away from me everything that I have today—my company, my products, my staff, and even my bank account—and leave me only with the email list I have as of now, I could still make multiple six-figures per month. How? Because I have millions of subscribers on my current email list. As I'm writing this, over the last 30 days, 247,929 unique people have read my emails. That's over 200,000 people who have also seen my offer. To put that in perspective, I recently flew to New York to attend a sold-out Drake concert in Madison Square Garden with almost 20,000 people in attendance. Drake, undoubtedly one of the greatest, most sought after artists of our time, would have to perform that concert *ten times* to get in front of as many people as I can get in front of just by clicking send on an email.

The value of an email list is profound.

It's also highly adaptable. As your business evolves, you will likely drop offers and add new ones, but you can bring your email list with you. If people don't like what you're selling anymore, they can unsubscribe. You can segment that email list, too, based on what people are interested in. In any email list, you'll have people who will be interested in new offers that are entirely different from the offer that first attracted their attention. You can find those people, add them to segments of your list, and sell to them.

Once you get into the freelance marketing space, you'll hear a lot of people who say that email is dead. The only reason they make that claim is because they want to sell you some other strategy, like a text message marketing tool or some other form of advertising platform (note that they're probably using email to market those offers to you!). But in actual fact, as I write this, email is the number one way to follow up with and generate revenue from your audience.

The bottom line is this: if you want to go fast, you could skip the email list step. But if you want to go far, then it's an absolutely essential tool in your arsenal.

A lot of people want to know which tech tools (i.e. autoresponders and funnel builders) they should use for their freelance marketing business. If you'd like to know exactly what tools we use, go to iiexplained.com to see our full stack of recommended software. In Chapter 10, you'll also learn more about email list management, but first, let's look at traffic and ads so you can understand how to attract your email subscribers in the first place.

Chapter 6

Traffic and Ads

If you're going to build a successful freelance marketing business, then you need to run ads. It is simply the fastest way for you to build your business.

To be successful, you need traffic. Remember: traffic means visitors (eyeballs) to your sales funnel and some of those visitors will trade you their email for more information about the products or services you're promoting (that's leads). So let's look at the two main types of traffic: free and paid.

Free Traffic vs. Paid Traffic

Paid traffic is when you pay to advertise on a platform. When you see ads pop up on your favorite social media sites, or on YouTube and your favorite streaming service, those are paid advertisements.

"Free" or organic advertising is when people promote their products or services on their regular social media profiles, simply by talking about what they have to offer and sharing stories of people who have worked with them. You see free ads everywhere online—TikTok,

Instagram, Facebook, and LinkedIn. Free advertisers put their offers in front of the audience that's already following them on their social platforms.

Another version of free traffic is SEO, or search engine optimization. Optimizing your website, blog articles, and other online content for search engines (like Google) makes it easier for people to find you when they're searching for something similar to the product or service you're promoting.

Both are good methods and both work. Free traffic is a great place for somebody to get started because chances are you already have some sort of an audience—friends or family members, people who follow you on social media, who may or may not be interested in a product or service that you have to offer. Simply talking about your offers on your platforms is a great place to start, and there are some decent strategies that you can use to get a jumpstart on this fairly quickly and start seeing sales relatively soon in your business.

Here's an example. A few months ago, a new client joined our community, went through our training, and decided to deploy a free advertising strategy. She was already familiar with TikTok, so she opened a brand new account and began promoting some of the products that we teach our clients to promote. During her second month on the platform, she earned $41,000. As I write this book, she has made about $40,000 a month for the last three or four months in a row. The beautiful part about her approach is that she has no ad spend. That $40,000 goes right into her pocket. Not a bad compensation for her time, right? Sidenote: You can get started the same way she did at iiexplained.com.

The challenge is that she's already reached her income ceiling. So far, she hasn't been able to exceed $40,000 a month because she's beholden to the social platforms and their algorithms, which can change without notice. Right now, the only way for her to get past that income cap is to add paid advertising into the mix.

I'm a fan of paid advertising because of one simple thing: time versus money. Which would you rather invest, time or money? Because in reality, there's actually no such thing as "free" advertising. You either pay for advertising with time or you pay with money. If you want free traffic, you have to pay with your time.

Let's break this down for a moment. What is the most amount of money that you can earn in your life? Infinite, right? Nobody knows. I mean, we're living in an era where people are becoming *trillionaires*. But how much time do you have in your life? Well, we know for sure that time is finite, and none of us knows how much time we have. And, once we spend it, we never get it back.

Successful people trade money for time. Unsuccessful people tend to trade time for money. The faster that you learn to trade money for time, the more scalable your business will be.

Here's another perspective: Do you know anyone who has 25 hours in their day? Any chance you have 366 days in your year? Of course not. If you rely on investing time in order to generate leads and customers for your business, there's automatically going to be a cap on your income.

But there's no cap on how much you can spend on ads in order to generate leads and customers. At the same time, you may not be able to invest large sums of cash on ads when you're just starting out, and that's okay. On a platform like Facebook, you can get started for as little as $5 a day, and then scale your ad spend as your income grows.

When I first started, I didn't have any money for ads, so I went through my bank statements and looked at all the places I was spending money. I called up AT&T and I lowered my cell phone bill to the most basic plan. I used to eat out every day for lunch, so I started packing my lunch more often instead of buying it each day. I was able to carve out an extra $5 a day to create a budget of $150 per month to spend on ads, which is the minimum amount I recommend for you.

In my first two months of advertising in the fall of 2012, I spent $300 to generate my first $25 commission. To some people, that might look like a $275 loss, but I was jumping up and down inside. I remember saying to myself, "Oh my god, it's real. I'm gonna be rich!" I realized that for $300, I had learned how to earn a commission, and if I could do that once, I could do it over and over again indefinitely. I was learning what was working.

I want to be clear though: this is not a get-rich-quick scheme. It's not like you're going to put money in a slot machine and have more money come out the other end. (Although I will say that most people do treat their business with a gambler's mentality, and that's why most don't succeed.) Paid advertising has a learning curve, and the first return on your investment comes in the form of lessons and information about what works and what doesn't. Everyone wants a shortcut to success, but there isn't one.

Money follows mastery.

Most people want to skip the mastery part and go straight for the money. Today, I make the money of a master, but it took me years to get here. I hope that by reading this book, you'll save years of trial and error. But to be clear, paid advertisements are not some sort of lottery ticket. At the same time, paid advertising is the fastest way for you to learn what will and won't work for your business, and once you learn those things, it's the fastest way to capitalize on what you learn.

It took me six months of paid advertising to transition from my first $25 commission to my first $10,000 month. That month, I spent $2,000 on ads, so I made about $8,000 in profit. That was also the same month I quit my job working in the coffee shop. By my first six-figure month, I was spending about $20,000 a month on ads in order to generate that $100,000 in revenue. In March 2017, when I had my first million dollar month, I spent about $300,000 on advertisements and made about $700,000 profit.

Note that I didn't work harder to make $100K versus $10K. And I didn't necessarily work harder to make a million dollars either. I simply had more leverage in the form of an infinite resource—money—versus the finite resource of time.

So if you want to keep your time attached to your income, just work a job. But I'm guessing that you're reading this book because you want to be able to earn an infinite income and have more time-freedom.

Intent-Based Traffic vs. Interest-Based Traffic

We can categorize most potential buyers into two types of traffic: intent-based and interest-based traffic. **Intent-based traffic** means you're attracting people who express an intention to buy something that is closely related to the product or service you're promoting. So, if somebody goes to Google and searches, "How to lose weight," they are showing an intent to lose weight.

If somebody goes to YouTube and searches for videos on how to invest in stocks, they're showing an intention to invest in stocks. If somebody searches Yahoo for information about investing in real estate, they have an intent to invest in real estate. If you place your ads in front of these people on these various search engines, that is intent-based advertising.

Generally speaking, intent-based advertising brings in the highest quality traffic you can get. These are people who are in the market to buy the products or services you're promoting—or your competitor's.

The challenge with this type of traffic is that your advertising costs are considerably higher because these platforms know that every visitor is worth considerably more. Because there's more competition and higher advertising costs, you've got to make sure that your products or services can sustain those costs.

Interest-based traffic refers to people who are more generally interested in topics that are related to your product or services. For example, if you're selling a product on meditation, you might look up some popular authors who have written books that recommend meditation. One that comes to mind is Eckhart Tolle. You could create a Facebook ad that targets people who are interested in Eckhart Tolle. And because they're interested in Eckhart Tolle, you also know they might be interested in meditation. One set of interests can be closely related to other sets of interests.

This audience's online activity simply shows they may be interested in meditation. But you don't know for sure whether they're in the market for a meditation program. They might be perfectly happy with their current meditation protocol. However you do know that, based on their interests, there's a greater-than-average likelihood that they would be interested in what you have to offer.

You can use the same strategy on YouTube to target people who follow or subscribe to certain channels that include content closely related to your offers. If you're selling a fitness product, you might find a channel that is all about fitness and target your ads to their subscribers. Again, you don't know if those people are actively in the market looking for a fitness program. But you do know that based on their interests, they show a greater than average likelihood of being interested in your offer.

It typically costs less on average to get in front of interest-based traffic because that market has a lower intent to buy—that's the trade-off. But both types of advertising are good, and you should learn both. We typically train our clients to start with interest-based traffic because it's more affordable, and I encourage you to start there too.

Pro Tip: What else is your audience interested in? Find out, and target those interests with your ads. You'll enjoy a competitive advantage and a greater return on investment (ROI).

One of the reasons I like interest-based traffic is that if you're willing to do the research on a platform that has interest-based targeting (like Facebook/Meta), you can find interests similar to your offer and target those people in your ads. For example, say you want to target people who are interested in weight loss. Facebook will show you other topics that people interested in weight loss are also interested in. For example, you might discover that people interested in weight loss also typically like a certain brand of toddler toys. Makes sense, right? People interested in toddler toys are likely to be parents who lack time and energy to work out. You may not be selling toddler toys, but you will still reach people who are interested in your weight loss offer.

It costs a lot less money to get your ads in front of those people because you're not going directly after weight loss, where all your competitors are bidding for attention. It takes a little extra legwork to do the research, and your ad copy needs to be a little bit stronger than somebody who's selling directly to a weight loss audience. But you get a competitive advantage, and a greater ROI.

Case Study

In our community, a bunch of us were selling a water ionizer product. One guy just started blowing up—he was selling close to ten ionizers a week. They were pricey machines, by the way, each one worth about $5,000.

Finally, he shared his secret: the keyword he used as his target interest was *beer*. That's it. He'd done the research and discovered that people who buy water ionizers also typically like beer. On top of that, you can't promote alcohol on Facebook, so nobody else was running ads for "beer" as an interest. His ads got shown to a far bigger audience for way less ad spend than the rest of us, and he was able to capture the attention of his ideal market with zero competitors.

All you need is a little creativity to increase your ROI and bypass your competitors.

Fixed Cost Advertising vs. Performance-Based Advertising

Fixed cost advertising means that you know exactly how much it costs you to get one lead and/or customer. When someone clicks on your ad and goes to your website or landing page, it costs you a specific amount (this is called the cost per click or cost per lead). You can also partner with other entrepreneurs who will allow you to email their list about your offer in exchange for a fixed cost per click. Once you know your costs per lead, you can figure out how much it costs you to get each new customer. For example, if your landing page typically converts at 25% (or a quarter of the people who visit your landing page give you their email) you can strike up a deal for a cost of $1 each time someone clicks on the email link. In this case, your cost per lead is likely to be close to $4. If you convert 3% of your leads into customers with your email follow up (very doable), you can estimate that it'll cost you about $133 ($4 divided by 3%) to acquire a customer. If your commission is greater than $133 per sale in this example, you're in the money!

Performance-based advertising, which represents the majority of advertisements out there, means that the cost of the advertisement fluctuates based on how it performs. This is called variable customer acquisition costs. Most social media platforms have something called CPM, which stands for "cost per thousand impressions." Based on the market or the type of people that you want to put your advertisement in front of, there's going to be a general cost range to get your ad in front of that audience.

If your advertisement performs really well, the platform rewards you. Why? Because it means your ad is less obtrusive to the audience it's being shown to, which creates a better user experience. When you're scrolling through Facebook, you want to see pictures of your friends, family, and things like the cool vacations that they're taking. You don't necessarily want to see an ad, right? But if you do see an ad that's closely related to things that you're interested in, you're more likely to click.

If your advertisement is well written and well thought out, has a compelling image and a strong hook, it will perform well; when it performs well, the platform will reward you by bringing down your cost per thousand impressions. If your direct competitor has an ad that doesn't perform as well, they'll pay a higher CPM.

A percentage of the people who see your ad will click on it and visit your landing page or website. A percentage of those people will also sign up to your email list, and a percentage of the people who give you their email address will also buy. Theoretically, the lower your CPM, the lower your cost per lead, and the lower your cost per sale (called cost per acquisition, or CPA).

I wouldn't say that one type of advertising is better than the other. You have to understand both so you can determine what's economically feasible for your business. But fixed-cost advertising opportunities are harder to come by and require more advanced skills in most instances. That's why I started out with performance-based advertising, and generally recommend some form of this strategy for beginners.

On the other hand, fixed-cost advertising is more advantageous in the long run because it's more stable and therefore is easier for you to predict the future economics of your business and make sure your business is more scalable. When a company uses a freelance marketer to sell their products or services for a predetermined commission, that's an example of fixed-cost advertising. The company knows exactly how much of its total revenue it will pay in commissions. If they pay you a 50% commission, their cost to acquire a customer is 50%, which is a much more sustainable business than somebody who relies purely on performance-based advertising, and whose acquisition costs fluctuate continuously.

For example, if you were a product owner and listed your products and services on affiliate platforms like ClickBank, you would have to build a funnel that converts, but if you can get your system to work, you will have a fixed customer acquisition cost because your affiliates drive all your revenue for you. The downside is you have no control over whether or not those affiliates come or go, so your revenue might go up or down. But the cool thing is that for the most part, your margins will stay intact. The other advantage is that you only pay when you make a sale, whereas if you advertise on a platform like Facebook, you pay whether you make a sale or not.

Fixed-cost advertising strategies are few and far in between these days, and they typically take a lot more skill for the average person to utilize. But lucky for you, you don't have to start from scratch. We offer a fixed-cost advertising strategy for our clients when they start working with us. All the information you need to get started is right here: iiexplained.com.

Put simply: If someone else is sending you a customer, you have fixed customer acquisition costs. If you have to acquire your own customer, you have variable customer acquisition costs. At the end of the day, it all comes down to figuring out what it costs you to acquire a customer and then choosing the right strategy for your business.

We've already talked about the best offers to start with if you want to win as a freelance marketer, but in the coming chapters, you'll learn how to put your own spin on those offers to stand out against your competition. Are you ready to learn how to create, test, market, and scale offers that can make you millions? Great! Keep reading.

Part 3

Conversions

Chapter 7

Copywriting

Copywriting is the art of selling via the written word. Everywhere we look, we see copywriting in action. We see it in commercials and infomercials we watch on TV or online; we see it in advertisements when we open the paper, throughout our social media feeds, and on every website we visit. Copywriting is words that have the specific intention of selling us a product or service or persuading us to take a certain action, like calling a hotline, signing a petition, or joining a community.

I like to say that *copy is king*. If you miss 80% of the mark in your overall advertising and marketing strategy but you have great copy, you will convert readers to buyers. This skill set alone has probably made me tens of millions of dollars and it is something that fascinated me early in my career.

I started in the industry in 2012, and by 2013 I was all over the leaderboards as one of the top freelance marketers for a particular offer that I was promoting. The company whose offer I was promoting was hosting an event in Chicago, Illinois, and two weeks before the event started, I got a random phone call from a woman named Tracy, who was calling on behalf of one of the biggest affiliates in the industry at the time.

"We see that you've been producing considerable results," Tracy said. "Toby would like to meet you in person and invite you to a private dinner."

I knew Toby was making $60,000 to $70,000 per month, which was an ungodly amount of money to me at that time. So of course I said yes.

The dinner took place on the last night of the event, at the same time as the big afterparty where all the affiliates were celebrating. Instead of joining them, Tiani and I joined Toby for dinner at a nice steakhouse across the street. I still remember walking in—it was one of the first times in my life that I'd been in such an opulent restaurant. The host guided us through the restaurant to a private room at the back. She slid open the doors and showed us to the bar.

"It's an open bar, so feel free to order anything that you'd like," she said, then indicated a table laid out with various cuts of beef, each with a certificate to show where the animal had been raised. "These are the cuts we have available this evening, so you can select yours."

Tiani and I were new to this type of dining experience, so we ordered a drink and chose our cut of beef. Then I turned and saw Toby sitting at a table. He waved at me and pointed to the seat right next to him. I walked over, sat down, and we started to talk.

"So Keala," he asked me, "what are some of the biggest challenges you're facing right now in your business?"

"Well, I'm not sure what to focus on next," I said.

He asked me if I'd gone to the party across the street, and I told him I'd stepped inside for a minute but didn't want to be late for dinner.

He responded with a story that changed my life forever.

> My wife and I got there early, and the co-founder's brother was there. He's a hypnotist. My assistant is also here with us, and she has cancer. She's going through treatment right now. The hypnotist asked her if she wanted to go upstairs and do a therapy session, and she agreed. So all four of us went upstairs to his hotel room and he started the session.
>
> Before we knew it, my assistant was fully under hypnosis. He walked her through his process, asking her to tell us what she was seeing. She started to describe the eye of God looking down on her from the sky. And she was interpreting that as God is letting her know that he was watching out for her. Next, she described feeling an intuitive nudge to turn on a water faucet. In the corner of the room that she built in her mind, she could see a sink. She walked over to the sink, turned on the faucet, and a black sludge poured out.
>
> As she was describing that to us, she began to cry and said she was seeing the cancer leave her body. By this time, all four of us were in tears. I mean, she was having a real emotional experience that was extremely visceral for her, even though it was all happening in her mind. When she came out of the trance, she was still crying—we were all touched by witnessing her experience.

Toby stopped for a moment and leaned in close to me. "What caused that experience?"

"I don't know—emotion?" I said.

"No. Words, Keala. Words created that experience. If you want to be a master of marketing, master your words."

Nobody had ever explained the power of words so profoundly to me before. The woman's entire experience was created by words alone. That's what put her under hypnosis and created the experience of seeing her cancer pour out of her body so she could heal. By the way, she is cancer-free today!

I was hooked on the art and science of copywriting from that moment on. I bought every book about copywriting I could get my hands on. I even bought books on hypnosis to learn some of the techniques that I've since used in my copywriting.

Copywriting taps into the power of words. It is both the science and art of using words in a way that sells—whether that "sale" is a monetary transaction or in the form of persuading someone to take a specific action that we desire. And as I said before, in my world, copy is king. The reason I say that is because I have made some massive mistakes in my marketing, and do you know what saved me from failed campaigns? My copy was phenomenal.

You could do just about everything else wrong but crush your copywriting and you will succeed. Let's learn key copywriting components that will make you one of the most persuasive and influential people that you know.

The Unique Mechanism

Every business is in the business of solving problems for a customer. But when you can identify the particular way that you (or the product you're promoting) solve a problem for your customer that nobody else in the marketplace has access to, then you differentiate yourself from all the competitors in the marketplace. That's your unique mechanism.

Big brands do this, and will even trademark, patent, or copyright their unique mechanism. Nike has patented the soles of their shoes, for example. They claim to use a unique technology, similar to the way mattress companies claim they each use a unique sleeping foam or way of layering springs and padding that fulfills the promise they make for a better night's sleep. The unique mechanism solves a customer's problem in a way that nobody else can, and therefore makes other offers in the marketplace invalid in comparison.

One of the best examples of a unique mechanism that I can think of is celebrity fitness trainer Tony Horton's P90X® fitness program. Depending on your age, you might remember the infomercials from the early 2000s, when P90X® took the world by storm, selling more than 4 million DVD copies by 2013. What's interesting about this fitness program is that it did not promise a simpler, faster, easier solution to weight loss, which is the concept most other products are designed around.

Instead of promising six-minute abs, or seven-minute workouts like their competitors, the P90X® message to the market was that this program was extremely hard and most people shouldn't try it. They took a completely different approach, which worked because of their unique mechanism: something they called "muscle confusion."

In their infomercials, they claimed that the reason people don't get results in a typical workout program is because the body adapts to the workout at some point and plateaus. Muscle confusion was their solution to this problem. In order to get better results—faster weight loss and a shredded body—their workouts changed dramatically on a regular basis to "confuse" the muscles, causing the body to continue to adapt.

What's most interesting about their marketing is that muscle confusion wasn't a new concept—in fact, most workout programs at the time were using the same concept to help people get results. It's just that nobody ever coined a catchy phrase to describe it.

By using the term, "muscle confusion," P90X® marketers were able to convince the market that they had found the secret to finally getting that shredded body the customer desired—a secret missing from all other available workout programs. And it sold like wildfire.

You can tap into this power in your offers, too. A unique mechanism doesn't have to be an original characteristic, concept, or feature that no other program or service has. Remember, "muscle confusion" was simply a new name for a convention that already existed. Your unique mechanism can be as simple as a phrase that you coin for some aspect of your solution that nobody else is using.

A great example of this is the book you are reading. Here's a big reveal: "freelance" marketing is exactly the same as affiliate marketing. I simply coined a unique name for it. See, back in 2016 when I launched my coaching business and first courses, I didn't want to call my training *affiliate marketing* because anybody who Googled the term would get a list of all my competitors in the marketplace at that time. I didn't want my prospects to go comparison shopping. So I coined the phrase *freelance marketing,* and used it in all of my copywriting. At the time, nobody else was using that term, so if someone Googled it, the only person they found was me.

To the average consumer, it seemed like I was the only person teaching this freelance marketing concept. A few years later, when my YouTube videos had 200 million views, other marketers started to adopt the term. But right from the start, freelance marketing was my unique mechanism. That's how I eliminated my competition and dominated my market. My sales went from zero to $20 million in just twelve months.

That's what a few simple words can do for your business.

The Big Domino

Closely related to the unique mechanism is the Big Domino Statement. As far as I know, this was coined by my friend Russell Brunson in his book *Dotcom Secrets*. The Big Domino Statement summarizes our unique mechanism and message to the market. It goes like this:

> If I can make most people believe that [*my new opportunity*] is key to [*what they desire most*] and is only attainable through [*my specific vehicle*], then all objections become irrelevant and they must invest.

For example, my Big Domino Statement is:

> If I can make most people believe that freelance marketing is the key to having a six or seven-figure business while also having the free time to enjoy life, and it is only attainable through my program, Fullstaq Marketer, then all other objections are irrelevant and people must invest.

The purpose of the Big Domino Statement is to capture and summarize your unique mechanism into a succinct way of delivering your message to the market. Whatever offer you're promoting is your unique solution to what the customer ultimately desires. If you can convince them that the only way for them to get their hands on your unique solution is through your product, service, training, or program—then all bets are off and they must buy.

Enter The Conversation In Your Prospect's Mind

One of the key components of great copy is that readers don't even realize that they're being marketed to. The writing is almost hypnotic, so readers are in a trance from the moment they start consuming it.

The roots of this concept go back to the early years of hypnosis when it was believed that in order to hypnotize someone, you had to shut down their conscious mind in order to access their unconscious or subconscious mind. Think of the classic hypnotist swinging a pocket watch back and forth saying, "Close your eyes, you're getting *verrry* sleepy," until the subject fell into an unconscious trance state. In later decades a new form of hypnosis, called "neuro linguistic programming" became popular. NLP is the ability to hypnotize yourself or others while remaining completely conscious.

Science has discovered that we are all in a trance, or "hypnotized" all of the time. We're hypnotized by what we hear on the radio, what we watch on television, and what we see on social media. During the pandemic, for example, people were in the, *"Oh my god, there's a pandemic!"* trance. Then came the, *"I have to wear a mask and get a vaccine"* trance. Some were also in the, *"It's a government conspiracy and all vaccines are a scam!"* trance. All of these dialogues echoed through social media, through our circle of friends, through mainstream media, and through streaming platforms that we watch for entertainment. And these dialogues created a sort of trance that we, as a society, adopted as our own reality.

In a real way, none of us experience reality—we only experience our version of it. Whatever "trance" someone is in, there's already a conversation happening in their mind. They might be sitting in traffic, in their *"on the way to work"* trance, or the trance they're in while they do their job every day. There's the trance of cooking dinner after work or of doing homework with the kids.

We enter these states largely unconsciously because they've become so habitual. And in these trances, there's a certain conversation taking place in our internal monologue. A great piece of copy penetrates directly into that conversation happening in your prospect's mind.

Here's an example. If I wanted to write a great radio advertisement, I might start with, "If you're sitting in rush hour traffic right now on your way to work…did you know…?" People who are sitting in rush hour traffic on their way to work hear those words and get pulled in without realizing they're listening to an advertisement. Why? Because my words didn't interrupt their thought process. I've simply joined a conversation already happening in their minds.

In the early years, one of my best-performing Facebook ad campaigns started with a headline that read,

If you're scrolling through Facebook right now…you might want to take a moment to read this.

I literally captured prospects in the trance they were in and entered the conversation as though I could read their minds. It stopped the scroll and brought in new leads.

Think about your prospects. What trance is your ideal prospect in? How do you enter the conversion in their mind in a way that is so unobtrusive they don't realize you entered it? These trances can be both specific and personal to your ideal prospect, or market-wide. Personal trances include things like someone wanting to be a better leader, someone who is in love, someone looking to get wealthy, or someone who wants to start or grow a business. At all times, these people are having a conversation in their minds.

When an entire market is in the same trance, it's a lot easier to enter the conversation. A great example of a market-wide trance is a recessionary economy. In a recessionary economy, people start thinking about how to protect their money, create additional income, and protect their jobs. In a recessionary economy like we had in 2009 and 2010—and like the economy we're segueing into as I write this book in 2023—it's a lot easier to market and sell because everyone is having the same conversation. It becomes easy to run advertisements that enter the conversation. Your copy might begin with headlines like:

How to create a recession-proof income.

How to create a secondary income to protect yourself against the recession.

How to get wealthy during a recession.

A lot of people make the mistake of thinking that in these sort of major market shifts, marketing opportunity has diminished. But in reality, money never stops moving—it simply flows in different directions. In the pandemic, money flowed toward vaccines, masks, online shopping, and home delivery. In a recession, money moves toward things like saving, investing, financial advice, and business opportunities.

Can you identify trends or overall themes in society or the economy that might encompass the prospects in your market, especially in relation to the product you are promoting? If so, it's great to call that out in your advertising. If you follow the conversations your ideal prospects are having, then you can follow where the money is going. And your prospects will be receptive to your messaging because you are speaking about topics they're already interested in learning more about.

Overcoming Objections

Most people in sales think that objections are natural. But I think that if your prospect has any objection to the product or service that you're promoting, you did a bad job of selling.

That belief has made me obsessive about trying to overcome every possible objection with my copy before a prospect even brings up the objection. Whether I'm promoting my product or service or someone else's, I design my ad campaigns and other marketing material to dissolve the most common objections any prospect might have. There are really only a handful of common objections that exist. They're all some variation of:

1. Does it work?
2. Will it work for *me* specifically?
3. Time
4. Money

You may come across some unique objections, but by and large, most objections fall into these four major categories. The goal of strong copy is to overcome these four main objections *before* the call to action. First off, your copy needs to provide proof that the product or service that you're promoting has gotten results for you and/or other people. Include stories about people similar to your ideal customer avatar. If your prospect is 50 years old and you convince them that your product or service works, but all they see in your testimonials and ads are 20 and 30-year-olds, they might assume that it won't work for them.

Identify your prospects' potential objections and then use those in your marketing. To help you address all possible objections, think about the "*even if*" questions your prospect may have. For example,

"Would this work for me *even if* I have very few tech skills?"

"Would this work for me *even if* I dropped out of high school?"

"Would this work for me *even if* I have no experience at all?"

"Would this work for me *even if* I've tried a hundred things like this before and none of them have worked?"

In your marketing material, address as many of these questions as you can.

"This could work for you *even if* you feel like you've tried everything else out there."

"This could work for you *even if* you feel you're too young for people to take you seriously."

"My fitness program will help you lose weight and get stronger *even if* you've never set foot in a gym before."

Then, there are time and money objections. If somebody says, "I need to talk to my spouse," that might be expected for a $10,000 offer, but is it likely they need to talk to their spouse to make a buying decision for a $10 product? No. That would be a money objection, not a spouse objection.

Another common objection is time. "I'm not sure I have the time for this." Most people don't have a lot of spare time, so you have to show people that they don't need a perfect environment to be successful.

Typically, I like to use a strategy called **risk reversal** to address time and money objections. I reverse the risk by pointing out that their objection is the reason they must buy.

If the objection is, "I don't have time for this," your copy will point out that the risk of them NOT buying is that they'll never have time for the things they love. If their objection is money, your copy points out that if they don't find a way to afford your product or service, they'll never get to a place where they can afford the things they want. The obstacle, then, becomes the reason they must seize the opportunity you've put in front of them.

Here's an example. A few years back, we promoted a cryptocurrency investing newsletter. In a seven-day promotion, we pulled in about $1.2 million in sales using risk reversal marketing to address the time and money objections, which are the two most common for people interested in investing in cryptocurrency. In our webinar presentation, emails we sent, and sales page copy, we flipped those objections around.

> If you feel like you don't have time to invest in cryptocurrency, isn't that exactly the reason you absolutely *must* invest in cryptocurrency—so that you can buy back your time, your freedom and your liberty?
>
> If you feel like all you have time for most days is to go to work, take care of the family each night, pay the bills, and go to bed, then when are you ever going to find the time to enjoy life if you don't start learning how to create an income passively while you sleep?
>
> This is why you must invest in cryptocurrency: to buy back your freedom. Our newsletter can teach you how.

We did the same thing with money. People had the perception that all cryptocurrency was like Bitcoin, which at the time, required a minimum investment of something like $7,000 to $10,000 to get started.

If you feel like you don't have enough money to invest in cryptocurrency, you can start with as little as a dollar.

> And if you feel like you don't have enough money to invest, then you need this product more than anyone. Because what else are you going to do to change your financial situation? Where else are you going to cash in on an opportunity this

> big? This would be like buying Apple stocks when shares were selling for a dollar.
>
> Are you going to let this opportunity pass you by as well?

In other words, if people lack time, your copy should show them how your product or service gives them time back. If they lack money, show them how your product or service helps them make back their investment and more.

Features vs. Benefits

When trying to sell a product or service, many marketers spend too much time talking about the features. But the truth is, nobody cares about the features. What they care about are the *benefits* of the features. How will your offer change their life? How can this product or service help them make more money, save more time, create more happiness, and find more fulfillment?

Nobody ever wants to buy a drill. What they want is a hole in the wall. And I would say that it goes even deeper. What they really want is for their spouse to stop nagging them about hanging the family portrait. That's what they want. They want *peace*. So, they go out and buy a drill to put a hole in the wall to hang a family portrait—all to get their spouse to leave them alone about it.

The best benefits are *emotional* ones. You want to drive home the emotional benefit that you're trying to provide for your customer. You may help them get more certainty, clarity, happiness, fulfillment, love, or joy—this list of emotions is based on whatever the end result is that you are trying to provide for your consumer. In great marketing, you may talk about the features if you find it necessary, but don't forget to tie in the benefits those features bring.

A great way to do this is by using a two-word phrase: *so that*. Use the words, "*so that*" as a trigger to help remind you to show your prospect the benefits—especially the emotional ones—of the features in your offer.

> "When you buy *XYZ* course, it includes 140 on-demand video lessons *so that* you never have to worry about how to solve these problems in your business again.
>
> The 1:1 access to our coaches will help you approach your business with the confidence, clarity, and certainty necessary to lead *so that* you're extremely confident in your sales process."

When I first started writing copy, I struggled a little bit to distinguish between a feature and a benefit. It helped me to remember that features are the measurable components of your offer; they could be 140 hours of videos, 15 lessons, or two hours of 1:1 coaching. But the benefits are the unquantifiable emotional impact that those features have. Certainty, clarity, joy, gratitude, fulfillment, alignment, freedom—these are the emotions people will feel as a result of buying your product or service. If you can find a way to skip the minutiae of your features, you'll make it easier for your prospect to see the benefit of buying your product or service.

This is important because *all buying decisions are emotional.* We make decisions to buy based on emotion, and then rationalize it later. This is a major component of good copywriting. Poor marketing tries to rationalize the purchase of the product or service. Instead, you want your prospects to start feeling those emotional benefits as soon as they enter the sales process. Help them imagine what it would feel like to have whatever emotional benefit they seek, and then show them how you can help them fast-track to their success.

You can use phrases like, "Imagine what it would be like if…" Or "Picture this." If you can paint a picture of their success, that mental image will enhance the emotions that drive their buying decision.

Six Basic Principles of Sales and Persuasion

The first book I read that helped me understand the psychology of sales and influence was *Influence: The Psychology of Persuasion* by Dr. Robert B. Cialdini. I highly recommend you read it if you want to go deeper into the six basic principles you're about to learn. For now, let's review a summary of each so that you can implement these principles in your marketing immediately.

Principle #1: Commitment and Consistency

We typically want to be seen as following through on our commitments. In fact, whenever we take action, we show a level of commitment, and we like to be recognized for not being a quitter. There are no awards for quitters in this world—that message is ingrained in our minds.

In marketing, we can capitalize on this fundamental part of human nature. Our aim is to create micro-commitments from our potential prospects. For example, if you create a Facebook ad and your ideal prospect stops and begins to read it, they've made a micro-commitment. If they have to click on your ad in order to see the entire text, that's another micro-commitment. If they click on the advertisement and go to your landing page, they've made yet another micro-commitment. They make more micro-commitments if they begin to scroll your landing page to consume the content, watch a video, etc.

The further you can pull your readers into making these micro-commitments, the more likely it is that they will buy in the end. In marketing, always tell your prospect what to do next. This is your call to action, or CTA. With every step, you ask your prospect for one micro-commitment which leads them to the next. And the more commitments you ask them to make before you get to the sale, the more likely they are to buy.

Why? Because people want to be seen as consistent with their commitments. Another term for this is the **sunk cost fallacy**. The longer someone engages with a piece of content, an idea, a person, or an authority—the more time and energy that they devote to a specific thing—the more they feel they must stay committed to it. Why? Because if they quit, they'll feel they've lost the time and energy they've already invested.

Think about it. I mean, for crying out loud, we spend our entire lives just trying to stay alive, and yet dozens of cult leaders have led people all the way to committing voluntary suicide. There might be individuals or even groups who stop to think, "Wait—am I really on board with all of this?" But they've already devoted so much time and energy to the cause that they can't convince themselves to turn around and go back the other way.

Commitment and consistency can also look like getting people to engage with your emails or your posts on social media, read your blog posts, watch your YouTube videos, listen to your podcast, or consume any other piece of content that you create to further ingrain them into your ideology. But there is a balance here. If you ask for the commitment too long without asking for the sale, you will eventually encounter diminishing returns.

This is where marketing becomes an art form. A great marketer knows exactly how many micro-commitments they can ask their prospects to take before they ask for the sale. There's no scientific way to measure this—at least not that I know of. It really depends on your audience, the type of offer, and their current level of awareness (as covered in Chapter 5). If you want to go further down this road, we have resources to give you massive shortcuts. Visit iiexplained.com to learn more.

Principle #2: Reciprocity

Reciprocity simply means that when someone does something good for us, we want to do something for them in return. As marketers, we can use this natural human characteristic to increase sales by giving value for free before we present our offer.

If you think about it, you've probably experienced the law of reciprocity many times. Have you ever bought something in a store simply because you were so well taken care of by the staff that you almost felt guilty about walking away without buying at least one small item? That's the law of reciprocity in action. I once bought an exotic car simply because the salesperson at the dealership was so good to me! True story.

During the pandemic, I was looking for a Lamborghini at a fair price and I approached a sales professional I had worked with before. I mentioned that I was looking for a Lamborghini with less than a thousand miles on it and that was not insanely overpriced. Each week, that salesman would send me details about a car that he'd found. He knew it wasn't exactly what I was looking for, but he wanted me to know that he was doing the research and looking out for me.

One day he sent me a Lamborghini that fit some of my criteria, but not all. I didn't necessarily like the color or the interior. In fact, there were a lot of things that I didn't like about that car. But he had worked so hard to find it, and given me such a high quality of service that I bought it anyway. I spent $305,000 buying a car because of the law of reciprocity!

Do not underestimate how powerful this tool is.

It's no mistake that when you go into a high-end store, the sales clerks will ask you if you'd like a glass of sparkling water or even champagne. They know that by giving you something for free, you're going to feel the need to give something back.

I like to start giving free value right from the first point of contact. I have found the law of reciprocity to be the most effective when my ideal prospect learns something from the advertisement alone. I've probably spent in the ballpark of $30 to $40 million on ads that provide real value. And when a prospect clicks on my link, I typically offer them something else for free on my landing page. This creates an experience similar to shopping in a high-end store.

If you can create an advertisement that doesn't just interrupt someone's online experience but creates some sort of ah-ha moment, you're much more likely to earn their business. You might give away a short online course, a webinar or virtual summit, a five-day challenge, or a helpful resource like a recipe book or printable planner. By doing that, you earn trust. Your prospect becomes more committed to the process. They sink further into the ideologies and beliefs with which you're indoctrinating them. This compounding effect increases the likelihood that they will eventually convert to a paying client.

Principle #3: Social Proof

Long before we had written words and language, people knew that foraging in the woods and hunting alone meant the odds of survival were minuscule to none. As a species, we've learned that in order to survive, we must belong to a tribe.

Today, humans still have a powerful drive to belong to a tribe. We look to others for cues on how to behave and take action based on what others are doing. Recently, I read about a young man who hired his own camera crew and paid people to come up and ask him for photographs and autographs as he walked around the city. Before long, total strangers wanted a photo and autograph with him too. He'd also hired people to pretend they didn't know who he was, and ask the strangers, "Hey, who's that guy you just had your picture with?"

The strangers would say, "I don't know, but I got his autograph!"

That's social proof. Seeing others take a certain action is proof enough for us that we should do it too.

You can use social proof in marketing by sharing stories about other people—stories of people who bought your product and achieved the result your prospect seeks. It's important to find people who can give testimonials about their success with your offer so that you can share those stories with your audience. The more social proof that you can show, the fewer your prospect's objections, and the more irresistible your offer becomes. When fear of missing out kicks in, your prospects will start imagining the possibilities they might miss if they don't jump on the bandwagon.

Principle #4: Liking (The Know-Like-Trust Factor)

People tend to buy from people that they know, like, and trust. Let me be clear: I've sold hundreds of thousands of products to hundreds of thousands of customers, almost none of which knew me personally in real life. They only *felt* as though they knew me from reading my sales funnel content, watching my videos, attending my presentations live, and reading emails I sent them. You are not limited to a warm market. You simply need a sales process or marketing funnel that allows your prospects to get to know you, like you, and trust you even if they never meet you in person.

Several factors are at play here. One is, undeniably, physical attractiveness. This is why oftentimes marketers will hire an attractive model or buy stock photos of a person who appeals to whatever society finds attractive. The Kardashians are a great example. Do you think that the Kardashians are famous because they're extremely talented, smart or savvy business people? No. Arguably, they might be savvy business people, but they are rich and famous mostly because they are attractive. Whether we want to admit this or not, physical attractiveness plays a role in likability.

We also tend to like people who are similar to us. The person most likely to buy from you is the person who is most similar to you. If you are the face of the product or service that you are promoting, the more you can share your similarities with your audience, the faster they will know, like, and trust you—and therefore buy from you.

A great example is a woman named Megan who joined our community in March of 2023. In May, she actively started marketing the products and services we recommend in our vertical selling system. (To learn more about that selling system, go to iiexplained.com.) To date, she's made $300,000 in just a few months. If you watch her content on TikTok, it's no surprise why.

Megan is a typical young mother who, until she joined our community, was working multiple jobs to make a living. When she went live on TikTok to share her journey as a freelance marketer and started showing her results, she attracted an audience of people just like her—most of them struggling single moms looking for a way out of their tough financial situation. That's why, as the face of her marketing, Megan quickly built the know-like-trust factor with her audience, leading to rapid success in her business.

Compliments go a long way in your marketing, too. It's no secret that people love to get genuine compliments. The more you can get your prospects to feel good about themselves and the decisions that they're making through direct or subtle compliments in your marketing, the more likely they are to know, like, and trust you—and therefore buy. You can sprinkle compliments into each micro-commitment your prospect makes as they go through the steps in your sales funnel, by saying something like, "Congratulations on taking this next step! You're really serious about getting results. Here's what to do next." Or at the beginning of your video presentation or webinar, you might say, "First off, I want to acknowledge the commitment that you're making. Not everybody who sees this is willing to take action." These built-in compliments encourage your prospects to keep moving forward and build an affinity for you as the face of your personal brand or the brand that you're promoting.

Principle #5: Authority

Wherever we look in society and nature, there are hierarchies. The further up someone is in the established hierarchy, the more authority they have, and the more likely they are to build a following.

Simply put, people tend to follow authority figures, and authority figures come in all forms—like police officers, bosses, C-suite executives, and politicians. Titles establish authority, too. There are

PhDs and Esquires and MBAs and Executive Directors. But as a freelance marketer, you don't need to have the formal authority of a title or established position. Authority is baked into your role.

Take this book, for example. Consciously or unconsciously, you've already positioned me as an authority in your mind. Why? Because you saw my advertisement online—along with my face and name. You then downloaded this book, which tells you that I know enough about the topic to write a book about it.

Even if you're a total beginner and you're marketing somebody else's product or service, the fact that you are running the advertisements, building the audience, and promoting something on the internet to your email list automatically gives you authority. Several decades ago, if we saw someone on television, we likely attached authority to that person, whether or not they had credentials to deserve the pedestal we put them on. We do the same thing today with people on the internet. Whether or not your face and name appear in your marketing materials is irrelevant.

Principle #6: Scarcity

Earlier in this chapter, you learned that all buying decisions are emotional—a human tendency that is key to effective marketing. It's also key to understand that people are more motivated by fear of loss than by the promise of gain.

Opportunities are seen as more valuable when their availability is limited. We don't want to miss out on something. If you position your offer as limited, you will increase conversions. That might mean limiting availability or quantity or presenting the offer as a deal that is ending soon. In Chapter 9, you'll learn more about how to craft offers that take advantage of scarcity to increase conversions, but here's an example of how I experienced the power of scarcity recently.

I was interested in buying a Range Rover, but as I researched, I came across the Rolls Royce Cullinan, which was three or four times the price of a Range Rover. I wondered why they were so expensive. I mean, the Rolls Royce Cullinan is a beautiful vehicle, but not three or four times more beautiful than a Range Rover. I dug a little deeper and discovered that they only make a few thousand Cullinans per year, and each vehicle is handmade. They are limited in quantity, and that drives up the perceived value in the marketplace. Yes, this car is luxurious, quiet, and has nice amenities. But frankly, nobody would be willing to pay half a million dollars for the car if scarcity didn't exist.

Now, think about what will happen if you couple scarcity in your marketing with everything else you've learned in this chapter. If you have an offer that's limited, and your prospects see you as an authority that they know, like, and trust, you've given social proof, AND on top of everything else, you've already given away incredible value for free—chances are, your prospect will buy from you at almost any price.

There is time to develop your copywriting skills, but these six basic principles of sales and persuasion will give you a huge advantage right from the start. If you can combine all six persuasion principles into your copywriting, your prospects won't be able to resist buying whatever you want to sell.

Blair Warren succinctly sums up the key components of influencing your prospects to generate a sale in this quote from his book, *The One Sentence Persuasion Course: 27 Words To Make The World Do Your Bidding*:

"People will do anything for those who encourage their dreams, justify their failures, allay their fears, confirm their suspicions, and help them throw rocks at their enemies."

If you want an example of how these 27 words play out in real life, think of every successful political campaign you have seen. Winning candidates encourage people's dreams. They make us believe that anything we want in life is possible…"If it weren't for those damn Republicans (or Democrats) who keep getting in the way!"

Successful politicians justify your failures. "It's not your fault—the system is rigged against you!" They work hard to help you set aside your fears, too. "Don't worry, when I get into office, this is all going to change."

They also confirm your suspicions. Do you remember the famous moment when Donald Trump walked out of the White House and basically said, "Hey! Everything that you think they're doing in there, they are definitely doing in there." People loved him for it. He confirmed his followers' suspicions that yes, they'd been taken advantage of in the past. He's probably the most polarizing politician I've seen in my lifetime, but he deployed this tactic better than anybody else I've seen.

Politicians throw rocks at their followers' enemies.

"Yes, doctors aren't being honest with you."

"You're right, lawyers *are* trying to take your money."

"The healthcare system is corrupt!"

"The game of politics is slanted in the favor of the wealthy."

Politicians use One Sentence Persuasion in their campaigns to build a rabid audience of people who believe, "This character is going to be the one to save us!"

The same is true in marketing, especially if you're marketing as a personal brand. Think about your audience. Whatever their dreams—falling in love, finding a soulmate, getting rich, living healthier and happier, getting six-pack abs—your job is to encourage those dreams and let them know that it's not their fault they've failed to achieve them. They didn't have the one unique mechanism that your product or service has to offer.

You have to show them that although their fears may be real, once they buy your product or service those fears will go away. If their fear is that they don't have the confidence to approach people of the opposite sex, you'll tell them, "Don't worry. You're going to learn that inside our program."

If they're afraid they'll never be able to create intimacy with their spouse again, tell them your online course will teach them how to bring intimacy back.

Are they worried they won't be able to build enough wealth to retire comfortably? Well, you're going to teach them how to invest money. Take the time to understand your prospect's fears, and then use your marketing material to address them.

No matter the market, people are suspicious that a piece of vital information has been hidden from them, and that's why they can't get all the answers or secrets they need to get results. Confirm their suspicions that they've been lied to.

Use language like:

"None of the other trainers want you to know this."

"Doctors don't want to tell you this."

"Lawyers don't want you to find this out."

"Here's what the wealthy elite hope you never find out."

Everyone is trying to keep your prospect from what they want, except you. You're the knight in shining armor who's come to save them. And quite frankly, most people want to be saved.

They also want you to help them throw rocks at their enemies. It proves you're on their side. In your copy, say things like:

"You're right for not believing the medical system."

"You're right for realizing that the Democrats are trying to steal your wealth."

"You're right for believing that Republicans are racist."

Whatever the thing is that they believe, align your marketing to position you as an ally. But only do this if you can get behind their beliefs *authentically*. I can't stress that enough. Otherwise, you run the risk of being manipulative with your copy; I want to be clear: I never intend you to use the information I share in this book to manipulate people. I share it in the hopes that you will use it to *influence* people in your marketing so that you can achieve success as a freelance marketer. And there's a big difference between influence and manipulation.

Manipulation means encouraging someone to do something that they don't want to do, that isn't in their best interests or goes against their character, ethics, morals, or principles.

Influence means genuinely helping your prospects by persuading or encouraging them to pursue their own self-interests.

I've often heard people say that if you truly believe that the product or service that you have to offer will benefit your prospect, you should do everything in your power to get them to buy. I have also witnessed a plethora of narcissistic assholes use that same justification to manipulate people into buying something that they didn't need.

The purpose of this book is not to teach you ethics or morality—that's up to you. My purpose is to teach you the best tactics that can make you a lot of money. You now have a powerful set of tools at your fingertips. I hope you'll use these powers for good.

Chapter 8

How to Make More Money on Demand

What if you could do the same amount of work at your job that you're doing right now, but make eight times the income? Is that even a possibility?

Think, for a moment, how impactful it would be to be able to increase your income by that much. In the career or the field that you're in currently, what would it take for you to make eight times more money? Would you have to work eight times as many hours, eight times as many days, have eight times as many lifetimes in order to make that happen?

As freelance marketers, we 8x our income on a regular basis through a simple strategy called **split-testing**.

Split-testing is the practice of optimizing your marketing and sales material by running different variations of ads, sales pages, headlines, and so forth; and then measuring which of those variations created the greatest increase in conversions. Let me explain split-testing using a simple example.

Let's say you roll out your first advertisement on Facebook, spending just $10 a day, and you get a 1% click rate. That means one in every 100 people who see your ad actually clicks on the link and goes to your landing page.

Now, let's say that you run a second advertisement alongside the first. You add a budget of another $10 per day to that second advertisement, but it gets a 2% click-through rate. Well, now for the same amount of ad spend, you have twice as many visitors to your landing page.

Say your landing page is generating a 10% conversion rate, meaning 10% of the people who hit your landing page give you their email in exchange for more information. You decide to run a second variation of that landing page, with a new design and color scheme. You also tweak the headlines and the calls to action a little bit, resulting in a 20% conversion rate on that new landing page. The same amount of traffic is hitting your landing page, but now you're getting twice as many people to give you their email in exchange for your free offer.

All of those people are now on your email list. You decide to split-test your emails, too. You test different subject lines and different times of day when you send your emails to your subscribers. Through these tests, you take your average open rate from 10% to 20%. Now twice as many of your leads are opening and reading your emails. Those leads are obviously clicking through to see the offer that you're promoting.

Notice that you did not spend any more money on advertising—you're still spending $10 a day. However, just by split-testing your ads, you've got twice as many people clicking on them. And now you've doubled your revenue.

On the landing page, you again double your conversions from 10% to 20%. Now you're getting four times the amount of revenue. You also doubled your email open rate, which means you've doubled the consumption of your email marketing in your funnel. Now that's *eight times more revenue.* Without changing your offer or the product or service at all, and without changing the amount of dollars that you're spending on advertising, you just increased your revenue by 800%.

That's a massive increase in ROI on your ad spend. All of these numbers are extremely realistic. In fact, I even suggest that these numbers are conservative. Through split-testing, I have had advertisements go from a 1% click-through rate to as high as 5%. That's five times the income right there. My team and I have taken landing pages from a measly 10% opt-in rate all the way to a 40% and even 50% opt-in rate. With our email list, we took our open rate from 10% to over 60%. Again, all things being equal, that's six times the revenue.

You can increase revenue even more by split-testing the bonuses you pair with your offers (you'll learn more about bonuses and crafting your own offers in the next chapter). In reality, with a proper set of split-tests, it's not uncommon for freelance marketers to increase revenue from one funnel by thousands of percentages, not just 800%. And the value of split-testing in your business is that you make a ton more money for the same effort.

There are some key principles that set you up for success with split-testing. When it comes to advertisements, the thing that will increase your conversions most is the creative itself. As a friend of mine likes to say, "Design screams, copy whispers." Your ad design has a huge impact on the success of your ad, whether the creative is in the form of a video, an image, or a carousel of images. The next most important part is the headline on that advertisement, and third, is the call to action—the promise you make about what the person will receive when they click the link and go to the next step.

When it comes to landing pages and sales pages, the biggest difference also comes from design. That includes the elements on the page, the overall color scheme, and the look and feel of the page itself. An interesting thing to note is that most of the time, pretty landing pages convert less.

Once you nail down the top-performing page design, work the copy from the top down. Look at your headline, subheadline, and the copy of the actual sales medium on the page. Maybe you ask people to watch a video or a webinar. Whatever device you use to sell your audience, pay attention to the words you use. On a landing page, you'll also have some sort of a call to action, which is basically asking people to opt into your email list. On a sales page, the call to action is to buy.

When it comes to sales pages, the biggest thing that swings the needle is the offer itself. As you'll learn in the next chapter, your product or service is not your offer. Your offer is a combination of the products or services, price, bonuses, and terms—a combination of which you can split-test to get the best results. Once you have your offer figured out, you'll be ready to scale.

We've covered the basics, but split-testing is a scientific process and a robust topic I could write an entire book about. There are costly software tools in the marketplace that will help you split-test effectively, but it's not the easiest thing for a total beginner to deploy.

All of this might sound overwhelming, but through our vertical scaling system at Fullstaq Marketer, we have already done all of this for you. When you go to iiexplained.com, you can get access to our vertical selling system where you can sell the same products that we're selling using the same websites that we currently use to sell them, and the same traffic sources that we use to get customers.

We've already done the split-testing on these websites, pages, and traffic for you, which means you can shortcut to the end result of what would have otherwise taken you years to develop. We run hundreds of split-tests a year that have turned into thousands of percentages of increased revenue. Just for being here and reading this book, I'm handing these results to you on a silver platter.

Chapter 9

Crafting Offers That Make Millions

When it comes to crafting your offers, the first thing that is critical to understand is that a product is not your offer. Understanding this key distinction is what separates most entrepreneurs from a successful freelance marketer. As an affiliate, it's important to understand how offers and products differ; because once you realize that you are not hinged to the product that you're promoting, you can create compelling offers that are unique in the marketplace. This does two things:

1. **It differentiates you from everyone else in the market.** Even if there are tens of thousands of other affiliates promoting the same product that you're promoting, they will not have the same offer as you. And this creates exclusivity because the potential prospect can only get your offer if they buy through your unique affiliate link. You can use your creativity in crafting unique offers to stand out even in a noisy market.

2. **It radically increases conversions.** Here's what I mean. Imagine that you're driving down the street right now and you see a sign that says,

Going Out Of Business Sale. EVERYTHING MUST GO!
Up to 80% Off Store-Wide

You glance up from the sign and realize that it's a furniture store and you think to yourself, "Hey! I could use some furniture for the house. Why don't I pull in here? I've got a few extra minutes."

You pull in, park, and you walk around the store. Eventually, you find a lamp. You pick it up and think, "Hey, this would look good on my nightstand." You flip it over and see a little tag that says 80% off—marked down to $20 from $100. You say, "Well, for that price, I'll take it!" You go to the cash register, pay the $20 and walk out of the store with the lamp.

What did you buy? Most people would say, "Well, I bought a lamp." But that's not what you bought. What you bought was the offer. Let's break this down even further so you can understand why it's the offer you purchased, not the lamp.

A compelling offer is comprised of four major components:

1. Product
2. Price
3. Bonuses
4. Terms

Let's take a look at that offer again through the lens of these four components. What's the product? A lamp. What's the price? $20. What are the bonuses? Well, you got 80% off on that lamp. What about the terms? This is a going-out-of-business sale, which means that you have to act with urgency. You don't have time to kick this can down the road and maybe come back later when it's more convenient.

So, when you think through this process again, what actually happened? The moment you saw the sign, urgency was unconsciously triggered in your mind. You knew you didn't have time to come back later when you had more free time or when it was more convenient for your schedule. Now, had you not seen that sign and driven right by the store, you probably wouldn't have thought about shopping for furniture just then. Or, you might have thought, *"I should stop into that store sometime—maybe on the weekend or when I've got a day off."* But because of that sign, you realized that your options were limited. That's where the offer started.

Then when you walked into the store, you found a lamp that you liked. When you turned it over and saw that you could get a $100 lamp for 20 bucks, that sealed the deal for you. Again, that was the bonus. So, the lamp is what you got, but the offer is what you bought without even realizing it.

Now that you understand the difference between a product and an offer, let's look at these four components in more detail. As a Freelance Marketer you're selling someone else's product so you don't have control over the product and the price. However, you *do* have the ability to change the bonuses and terms as you'll see in a moment. By changing the bonuses and terms you can ramp up the urgency and/or scarcity of your offer which drastically increases conversions.

> **PRO TIP: People are more motivated by fear of loss than promise of gain.** It's an innate aspect of our human psyche that's nearly impossible to control. Generally speaking, people will act faster and spend more if they're afraid of missing out. Add scarcity and/or urgency to your offers and you'll radically increase your sales.

You build urgency into your offers by imposing a time limit—like the going-out-of-business sale in our example. This business might not exist next week or two weeks from now, so you'd better buy now! Scarcity, on the other hand, is based on supply. Oftentimes in advertisements, you'll see phrases like, "while supplies last." This is intended to show you that if you don't act quickly, the seller could run out of that thing that you're interested in. If the seller only has ten T-shirts to sell and you're buyer number 11, too bad! You're out of luck. Urgency and scarcity aren't entirely necessary in a good offer, but if you can add one or both, you will massively increase conversions. I can't emphasize this enough.

Let's look at a hypothetical example of how you might apply product, price, bonuses, and terms to create your own compelling offer. Let's say that you're promoting a Facebook ads course for $199. The course is designed to help entrepreneurs grow their businesses and increase sales by using Facebook ads to drive more traffic to their websites.

What bonuses would make this offer irresistible? The best way to add the right bonuses is to figure out why people might not buy, even though they are interested in your offer. What excuses do they make for not purchasing? One might be, "I've never run Facebook ads before. How do I know this will work for me?"

Another might be, "I've tried Facebook ads in the past and they didn't work. Why would this be different?" These are common objections, along with time and money objections. The right bonuses will eliminate those objections.

Say your first bonus is Facebook ad templates with a fill-in-the-blank formula that helps people create successful campaigns out of the gate. In this example, you want to create an additional bonus of a detailed breakdown of some of the best, most compelling ads that you've ever seen to help your buyers get their ads right the first time. You go through Facebook ads and capture some that jump out for you, and then do a detailed breakdown of what made these ads compelling. Now your buyers have examples of successful ads to model theirs after, plus your plug-and-play templates.

Next, you need to figure out what sort of terms you could offer in order to increase sales. One set of terms might be that prospects have to purchase by a deadline—say, this Friday. Now that you've packaged your product together with your bonuses and terms, you have a unique offer that will help your products stand out in the marketplace.

In your advertisement, your message to the market would be something like this:

> Want to grow your business, but tired of unpredictable sales and revenue? When you take action now and buy this Facebook ads course for $199, not only are you going to get the full value of the course, but for a limited time, I'm also going to throw in **10 Facebook ad templates** that you can follow.
>
> These fill-in-the-blank templates (valued at an additional $199), give you a cutting-edge advantage so you can rest assured that your campaigns will be successful *right out of the gate.*
>
> And as if that weren't enough, I'm also throwing in a **detailed breakdown of the five top-performing ads that I have identified on Facebook**, and I will show you exactly why these ads convert so that you can model the secrets from some of the best advertisers on the planet. This bonus is valued at an additional $199. That's a total of $597 in value for just $199! But **you must act by this Friday at midnight** in order to lock in these bonuses.

What your prospect sees is that they are getting $597 of value for $199. They're also saving themselves time because you're giving them ad templates, plus giving them a breakdown of some of the best performing ads. Your offer saves them both time and money by decreasing the likelihood that they will lose money on their Facebook ads. You've also created urgency because they must act by Friday at midnight in order to take advantage of your bonuses.

Can you see how we took a simple product priced at $199 and made our own offer out of it by adding $398 of additional value plus increased the prospect's desire to take action by limiting the amount of time they can take to "think about it"? Doesn't that sound a lot better than buying the $199 course alone?

You see, as an affiliate, when you understand that there is a massive difference between a product and an offer, you are free to be as creative as you want in building offers that set you apart in the marketplace. And by adding bonuses and terms, you dramatically increase your overall conversions.

One of the best ways that I like to promote offers is through follow-up emails. When we're promoting a product, over time we'll develop thousands of leads for that product. By the law of averages, we know that only a small portion of those people are going to buy that product the first time they see it, but they might be interested in new offers that we create over time. We already have those leads and subscribers on our email list, so we're not paying more money to get more; we're just extracting more value from the leads we already have.

Using the $199 Facebook ads course example above, you can follow up with subscribers on your email list. Here a few subject lines you could use in your emails:

Act now before it's gone!

Get this before it disappears forever.

Facebook ads course PLUS two limited time bonuses!

By creating urgency right in the subject line, your readers will know that if they're at all interested in getting their hands on a Facebook ads course, they'd better open your email immediately.

Example email:

> Hey,
>
> Obviously you already know about the Facebook Ads Course for $199, and I would hate for you to miss out on the value of this course. So I decided to sweeten the pot just a little bit.
>
> When you lock in your spot before **midnight this coming Friday**, I'm also going to throw in:
>
> **BONUS #1:** 10 Facebook ad templates to help you create successful campaigns *right out of the gate*. This way you never have to worry about being creative and writing great ad copy, because these are simple, fill-in-the-blank templates to help your ads perform. These templates *alone* are valued at $199.
>
> PLUS, I'm throwing in:
>
> **BONUS #2:** A detailed breakdown of some of the BEST Facebook ads I've seen recently, along with a clear explanation about why these ads are so effective. Why? So that you can steal the secrets of some of the best Facebook advertisers in the world, saving you time, money, and headaches in the process. This incredible resource is valued at another $199.

But I can't offer this forever. So if you want to lock in this $398 worth of additional bonuses—*that's $597 worth of total value for just $199*—you **MUST act by this Friday at midnight**.

Talk soon,

Your Signature

When you create a promotion like this for our email list, you'll obviously have a cutoff date. In this example, it's midnight this coming Friday. You will email that list aggressively until the deadline. If I were going to have a Friday deadline, I would either start the Friday before, or Monday of that same week at the latest. This way I have five to seven full days of promotion. You would likely email your list two to three times per day to ensure that as many people as possible on our list see the offer. Why? Because the frequency also increases the urgency for them to buy.

Pro Tip: As an added bonus for you, here's a look at one of my most compelling offers.

The offer is an online course that helps you start your own affiliate marketing business. I walk through all of the tools that you need to set up your affiliate business and show you exactly how to integrate those tools so that you can get up and running in as little as a few hours. We sell this course for $99.

Now, I know that one of the common objections people have in my market is, "Well, I've tried lots of different business opportunities before, but I always end up not taking action." So when I designed the offer, I wanted to design a bonus that would help people overcome procrastination.

Another objection is, "I don't know about this online course thing, I want to talk to a real person and get advice about how to make this work for me. And if it doesn't work, can I get my money back?" So our bonuses and our terms overcome all of these objections.

The first bonus that we offer is a product called Fullstaq Edge. In it, I share information that I've learned over the years that is scientifically proven to help people overcome procrastination.

Bonus number two is they have the opportunity to book a call with one of our advisors to have a detailed conversation about the best way to bridge the gap between where they are and the goals that they want to achieve.

And if they're not happy for any reason within 14 days we'll give them a full refund.

So now that we understand why we design the bonuses and terms the way we do, here's a quick breakdown of the offer:

- Product: Affiliate marketing online course
- Price: $99
- Bonus #1: Fullstaq Edge. Get your hands on the secret science of annihilating procrastination once and for all so that it never steals your dreams again.
- Bonus #2: When you act now, we'll also throw in a FREE 45-minute consultation with one of our advisors who will help you create a clear action plan to help you bridge the gap between where you are and where you want to go.
- Terms: If you're not happy for any reason within 14 days, not only will we refund every dime you spend, but you can keep the entire product for yourself. So yes, you could take advantage of my kindness, but that's how certain I am that you are going to love our product.

This offer alone has generated about $20 million for our company over the last six years. You can apply these same concepts to craft offers that will make you millions, too, especially when you combine this with the science of scaling, which we cover in the next chapter.

Chapter 10

Managing Your Biggest Asset: Your Email List

Email is the lifeblood of a freelance marketer's business. If you've been in sales before, you've probably heard the saying, "The fortune is in the follow-up." In the online world, we follow up via email.

The beauty of using an autoresponder is that you can send follow-up emails on autopilot. As you learned in Chapter 3, all you have to do is write your follow-up sequence once, and your autoresponder will automatically nurture your audience and generate sales.

Over my first few months as an affiliate marketer, I built up an autoresponder sequence that was more than 90 days long, which meant my leads got more than three months of emails from me even if I never sat at my computer and wrote another email again. Those emails were designed to give my subscribers reasons to buy my offer, day after day, no matter where I was or whether I was working.

As I write this book, about 247,929 people have read my emails within the last 30 days. For context, that's nearly 5 times some of the largest football stadiums in America. Let that sink in for a bit.

Take everything away from me except my email list and experience tells me that I would still make well over $150,000 per month simply by emailing other people's offers to that list. Talk about having an insurance policy!

Do you think that if you could get 100,000 people to see your offer, you might make some sales? (Hint, the answer is probably yes!) By now you understand how important email is, so let's talk about how to manage your list effectively to generate revenue for your freelance marketing business.

Deliverability

The first rule of email marketing is deliverability, which is how to make sure your emails reach the inboxes of your leads.

Have you checked your spam folder recently? No? Neither have I. But if you did, you'd probably find hundreds or even thousands of emails in there. You want to make sure your emails never wind up in anyone's spam folder. Avoid that at all costs! If you want people to open and read your emails, you need to get those messages in their inboxes in the first place.

These four things (in order of importance) determine whether your emails go into your audience's inbox or the dreaded spam folder:

1. IP reputation
2. Domain reputation
3. Content
4. Links

Let's quickly cover each.

IP Reputation

Your IP reputation is related to the unique IP address assigned to the server that you send emails from. Your email service provider (i.e. autoresponder) owns that server, so there is little that you can do to protect its reputation.

However, it's still important to understand how these work. On a basic autoresponder account you will have what's called a shared IP address. That means that a pool of email marketers are all sending emails from one server and using the same IP address. This is important to understand because you're basically adopting the email reputation of whoever sends emails from the same IP address as you. In other words, if other people are spamming their email list or sending non-compliant emails out to their list, they can potentially drag down your email deliverability even if you're abiding by all the rules.

However, a reputable autoresponder company takes steps to protect you as a user. If somebody in your shared IP address pool is breaking the rules, your autoresponder will know and likely kick them off of the platform. (By the way, if you want to know what autoresponder companies we recommend, we've got a full list of resources at iiexplained.com). Ultimately though, you don't have full control of your reputation. You can get a dedicated IP address from good autoresponder companies, but those are usually reserved for enterprise-level accounts and can cost a few thousand dollars a month. For the most part, they're not worth considering until you creep up to close to six figures per month in revenue.

Domain reputation

When you email-market to a list of subscribers, you can't use a regular Gmail or Hotmail account to broadcast emails to your list. If you try, your account will be shut down. Not to mention that you won't have any of the advantages of automation. Instead, you use an autoresponder. As part of the setup process you'll need to create your own dedicated email address for your business, which will likely be something like *yourname@yourdomain.com* or whatever you choose as your business name. Again, if you want instructions about how to do this effectively, we can help you set up your entire online business from scratch and get guaranteed results in just one weekend when you go to iiexplained.com.

By the way, don't overthink this. I literally own hundreds of domains at this point. You're not married to your domain name and you can pick these things up for as little as a couple bucks. They're cheap and you're likely going to end up owning dozens, if not hundreds of domains if you're going to be a successful freelance marketer. So don't overthink the name you choose to start out with.

The domain you buy and set up to send emails from is uniquely yours and will develop a reputation over time. Over time the major mailbox providers—like Gmail, Hotmail, Ymail, etc.—will assign a reputation to your domain based on the content of your emails and how people engage with them. Your content, thankfully, you *can* control. In short, the better the quality of your emails and the better the engagement rate, the higher your reputation will be with these providers and the more likely you are to land in your subscribers inbox.

Content

Content simply refers to the words inside of your email. That includes everything from the subject line all the way down to the signature that you use at the end of your message. Every word is read by the bots that mailbox providers use to ensure that each message is compliant and also to figure out which folder they belong in (i.e. spam, junk, the promotions tab in Gmail, etc.). You need to be careful about the content that you use in your emails. We'll talk more about content shortly, but first, let's look at links.

Links

As a freelance marketer, you're likely going to include links in most emails that you send. These links take readers to some sort of sales material designed to turn that email subscriber into a buyer. You may link to a webinar, a video sales letter, a static sales letter, or a landing page. It's important that you use links that are 100% unique to you. You'll learn more about this in a moment.

Now let's talk about how to use IP reputation, domain reputation, content, and links to your advantage. Again, we can't control IP reputation, but we can control our domain reputation, our content, and our links. Maintaining a solid domain reputation has a lot to do with your content. Plainly put, you want to stay away from spam trigger words. For example, try as you might, you're never going to get an email with the word *Viagra* into the inbox. It's far too risqué, so to speak. Sexual content, prohibited content, and other explicit material is largely forbidden by commercial mailbox providers. The bots are going to crawl every email you send and if they feel that it is a solicitation, they will likely put that in either a Promotions tab in Gmail or in the spam or junk folder, depending on which email service provider your subscriber is using.

By the way, if you're wondering what spam trigger words to stay away from, a short Google search will help you find a laundry list of words that you should refrain from using in your emails. The key point I want to make is that you want to prevent your email from sounding like a solicitation, even though that's exactly what it is! This can be a bit complicated and in-depth, which is why we offer training, mentoring, and coaching for folks who are interested in starting their own freelance marketing business from scratch. You can learn more about that at iiexplained.com.

You can't just use any old link that you find on the internet and send it out to your email list. Each link sent out by email is eventually assigned a reputation by Gmail, Hotmail, Ymail, and all the other ESPs. Those platforms constantly monitor links to make sure they don't violate their terms of service.

One of the big mistakes that early-stage freelance marketers make is they go to an affiliate network, like ClickBank, one of the biggest affiliate networks in the world, and they will find a product or service that they want to promote. With just a few clicks, you can get a generic link called a hoplink. That hoplink will have a core domain attached to it—it's whatever comes before the .com (or .net, etc.). On big platforms like ClickBank, there may be 10,000 other affiliates promoting that same product or service. If all those other affiliates are sending out the same generic link in their emails, they are already creating a reputation for that link. And if they are violating any of the major email marketing rules, they're likely harming the reputation of that link. In other words, if any other person is sending the same exact link that you are sending out, you don't have control over that reputation, which means you don't have control over whether or not your email gets into your subscribers' inboxes.

For that reason, professional freelance marketers use something called link shorteners, which convert long URLs into something simple and easy on the eye. Most link shorteners also allow you to track how many times people click on the link over a period of time. Off-the-shelf link shorteners like Bitly or TinyURL are not any better than the generic link that you get from ClickBank because all Bitly and TinyURL links are based on the same core URL. Anyone who uses Bitly, for example, sends out emails with links that contain "bit.ly" followed by a few random letters and numbers that differentiate it from other Bitly links. This means tens of thousands—maybe even millions—of people are also sending out similar links. Those tools have a reputation that's already been assigned to them, so again, you don't have any control over the deliverability of your emails.

Ultimately what you want is a link *tracker*, which is a tool that not only tracks how many people click on your link but also allows you to take any link on the internet and shorten it into a link that is unique to you. When you set up a link tracker properly, your link will be attached to a domain that you own. The only person who will ever send that exact link is you, which means you control the reputation of that link.

You want to have control over all four of these components—your IP address, domain reputation, your content, and your links—as much as possible because if you use something that anyone else is sending, they could be tainting your ability to get into your subscribers' inboxes and therefore *crippling* your income.

Open Rate Engineering

It's not enough to just get inside of your prospect's inbox. You want people to actually open and read your emails. If they don't open, they don't read. If they don't read, they don't click. And if they don't click your link, they're not going to buy anything from you.

Now that you know how to increase the likelihood that your emails reach your subscribers' inboxes, how do you increase the likelihood that people are going to open and read your emails? Here are a few simple rules to follow.

First, what do you think is the number one thing that causes someone to open an email? Think about how you treat your own inbox for a second. Why do you open some emails and not others? Oftentimes people think that the key is a catchy subject line. It's not. The number one thing that makes someone open an email is the *sender*.

If you wake up tomorrow morning to 100 emails in your inbox, obviously you're not going to read them all. But if one of those emails was from your mom or your son or a sibling, you'd probably open that email. It's not so much about what the email says but who sent it. This is why the most important thing you can do is to build a relationship with the people on your email list.

By itself, email relationship building is an in-depth topic—yet another reason why we offer courses and coaching to people who are serious about starting their own freelance marketing business. You can learn more about that at iiexplained.com. But in short, your goal should be to create the perfect mix between value emails and sales emails.

Value emails help your prospect learn or discover something, have an *aha* moment, or otherwise help them solve some portion of the problem that they face. This builds you as an authority, and over time, nurtures your audience to know, like, and trust you so that they want to read more emails from you. If you overdo value emails nobody will buy from you, but if you send too many sales emails without giving enough value, nobody will read your emails.

Finding that perfect balance is a bit of a dance. It takes time and skill to learn, which is why we invest so much time with our clients to help them master this process.

The subject line is the next thing that is most likely to prompt your reader to open your email. The best subject lines pique curiosity enough to get subscribers to open and consume. Here are a few types of subject lines that I like to use, with examples of each.

The Question Subject Line

The human brain wants to know the answer to every question. The moment your subscriber reads the question in your subject line, they will have a hard time not opening your email to find the answer. Here are some examples:

Did you know about this?

Have you seen this before?

Are you ignoring me?

What's the best way to [fill in the benefit they are seeking]?

The Trending News Headline

If something is popular or trending in the media, I might craft a headline around it. For example:

What can Jeffrey Epstein teach you about traffic?

The Trump and Russia scandal is nothing compared to…

What can Taylor Swift teach us about dating?

How To [Benefit] And [Benefit]

Examples:

How to end wrinkles and look younger

How to destroy debt and increase credit

How to build a business and have a life

[Number Of] Ways To Benefit

Examples:

Five ways to destroy debt

Seven ways to burn fat

Three ways to look 10 years younger

These examples will get you started, but if you want 80 more catchy subject lines to help you write emails that get opened and read, I've put together a resource that you can access by going to iiexplained.com.

Resending

You've learned how to make sure your emails are delivered, opened, and read. Now let's look at resending, which is a strategy that I taught myself over time to target certain segments of my audience so I can engineer the conversation I have with them. I use resending in two ways. First, I will resend an email to people who've opened my emails most recently. Secondly, I will resend to non-openers (use this sparingly, because it can cause problems!).

Here's how this works. Not every person that opens your email will read it. Think about it. Do you read every single word in all the emails that you get? No. Neither do your subscribers. They might open your email, decide it's a little too long for them to consume right now, and click away. When I'm promoting something to my list (especially if I'm promoting it aggressively), I'll set up an email to go out at 7 a.m. Pacific time, and then I'll do a search inside my autoresponder to find out who opened my email but did not click on the link inside. Because if they didn't click the link, it means they didn't see the sales material I need them to consume to convert them into a customer. This kind of search is called segmenting your list. It's fairly simple and straightforward to do in any autoresponder, but if you can't figure it out on your own, reach out to their support and ask them to walk you through it.

That afternoon, usually around 4 p.m., I'll send another email to subscribers who opened my email but didn't click. This time, my subject line will say something like:

Why didn't you watch the video?

Why didn't you register for the webinar?

Why didn't you take action?

Inside the body of the email, I'll write:

> Hey, I saw that you read the email that I sent out this morning, but you didn't click the link inside. Why not?
>
> I get that it might have been an inconvenient time for you, so here's your second chance. Go here to watch XYZ before it's too late: [Link goes here]
>
> Talk soon,
>
> *Signature*

Here's why this is such an effective email strategy. First, you're emailing people who've already proven that they open your emails, so you will likely get a high open rate—easily 40% or higher. High open rates improve your domain reputation, so by doing this effectively (and not overdoing it), you increase the likelihood that your future emails avoid the spam folders. The second reason this strategy works is that rather than just sending a blanket email to your entire list, your readers feel that you are speaking directly to them because you know they opened your email but didn't click the link. They're more likely to take the action that you need them to take.

It's important not to abuse this strategy, but if you implement all the strategies you learn in this book—you've crafted your own offer and are heavily promoting it to your email list—this is an exceptional way to drive more opens, more reads, and more sales from your email list.

Now let's talk about resending emails to non-openers. The first thing to note here is that you must use this *sparingly*. I only use it once, maybe twice, if I'm in a heavy promotional period, and here's why. This time, I'll ask my autoresponder to give me a list of all the people who did not open my morning email and send an afternoon email, giving me a second chance to get more eyeballs on my email.

My subject line will say something along the lines of:

Are you ignoring me?

Did I make you mad?

Why didn't you read this?

Inside the email, I'll play up the urgency and scarcity to encourage the reader to click the link inside. For example:

> Hey, I saw that you ignored the email that I sent you earlier this morning! I get it. Maybe it wasn't the right time.
>
> However, this is *so* important! I want to make sure that you don't miss your chance to take advantage of my special offer—which I know you'll love. Go here to learn more about *XYZ* before it's too late: [Link goes here]
>
> Talk soon,
>
> *Signature*

This works for non-openers for the same reason it works for openers—it's a dynamic way of having a specific conversation with a particular segment of your list. If a person opens your message, they'll feel like you're talking directly to them, which increases the odds that they will click on your link and see your offer.

A word of caution: when you resend to non-openers, you are emailing people who have proven that they do *not* open your emails. That means the open rate to this segment of your list is as low as 5-10% if you're lucky. This strategy works, but if you overuse it, you will hurt your domain reputation.

Cleaning

Once a month, I get rid of the excess baggage from my email list. These are people who don't open my emails and therefore are never going to convert into a customer. Let's face it: not all subscribers will buy something from you—it's just the way that things are. Most autoresponders charge a monthly fee based on how many subscribers you have on your list, so there's no use holding onto leads that are never going to give you a return on investment.

To clean my list, I do a simple search in my autoresponder for subscribers who have been on my list for more than 90 days *and* who haven't opened an email within the last 90 days. (It's important to use both criteria when you search for subscribers to purge.) These are leads who are never going to convert for whatever reason, so I delete them from my list.

You want to get in the habit of flushing your list on a regular basis. By removing the non-openers, you increase your overall open rate, which benefits your domain reputation. The end result is increased email deliverability. It also saves you money because you're not paying for leads that aren't ever going to buy from you.

Chapter 11

Scaling Your Business

One of the things that I appreciate most about having an online business is that it's predictable. What would it feel like to give yourself a raise any time you choose? Imagine how different life could be. With a freelance marketing business, you simply engineer it. This is scaling and, plainly put, it's the process of growing your revenue.

I quit my coffee shop job on Tuesday, April 16, 2013; when I did, I was terrified. Over the previous twelve years of my adulthood, I had quit so many jobs way too soon in order to pursue some harebrained entrepreneurial journey. How could I be sure this freelance marketing thing would be any different?

Well, it was different, right from the start. The biggest reason for that is I had a mentor and a community to lean on (hint: big success clue right there). With their help over the days and weeks to come, I developed a formula that helped me engineer increases to my income and lifestyle. The month I quit my job was the first month I earned $10,000 in my business. Within a few months, I hit $20,000 in monthly income, then $30,000 per month a few months later, then $40,000 per month soon after. The rest, as they say, is history. But the shocking thing about my rapid growth was that all I used to scale that quickly was a little fourth-grade math and some elbow grease.

If you've passed the fourth grade in school, surely you can use this simple math to engineer your growth as well. Let me explain. Imagine for a moment that you've been practicing the contents of this book for a little while. You've spent $500 on ads, generated 100 leads on your email list, and had your first $2,000 month in sales. Not bad when you consider that most bankruptcy filings could have been prevented with just an additional $300 per month of income for the household. But it's not an entirely life-changing income either. You're hungry. You want more. You calculate your living expenses and come up with a "fire your boss number" of $10,000 per month in sales. This is all the information you need to reverse engineer a plan to reach that goal.

et's break it down. To achieve your goal of $10,000 in monthly income, you first need to ask yourself how many leads you need in order to hit that goal. Looking at the numbers that you've generated so far, you've brought in $2,000 in sales from 100 leads. That means your average lead value, or ALV, is $20.

Next, take your goal of $10,000 and divide it by your $20 ALV. That equals 500 leads that you need to generate to hit your goal. Not easy, but not hard either. You've just broken down your big goal into something that's much smaller and more achievable.

So what do you need to do to generate 500 leads per month? First, take a look at what you know: you've spent $500 on ads to generate 100 leads. So $500 divided by 100 leads equals $5 per lead (that's your cost per lead, or CPL.) You take the 500 leads that you need per month and multiply it by $5, which means you'll need to spend $2,500 per month on ads to hit $10,000 in monthly revenue. Sure, that's a stretch in the beginning, and you won't get to the point where you can afford that overnight, but it is doable.

I don't know about you, but I don't live my life in months; I live day to day. So I like to break my big goals down into daily activities so that I know that if I just focus on doing this thing every day, I'll hit my goal. Think of it like this. Have you ever spoken to somebody who's on a diet? They don't say that they're eating 60,000 calories per month. Instead, they say that they're focused on eating 2,000 calories per day. Success is about making big goals small. So what do you need to do on a daily basis in order to get 500 leads at the end of the month?

Well, take that $2,500, which is what you need to spend in order to hit your goal, and divide it by 30 days, and that equals $83.33 in required ad spend per day. So all you need to focus on is getting your ad spend to $83.33 per day. That feels more doable, right?

Again, will it happen overnight? No—you'll get there over time by taking your monthly earnings and investing more and more of it into ads until you increase your ad spend to $83.33 per day.

Now, here's what's important. In this example, you just increased your earnings by 500% from $2,000 a month to $10,000 a month. But did you have to increase your workload by 500%? No, not even close. All you did was increase your ad spend from $5 a day to $83 a day. That's the difference between leveraging money in order to make money, versus using time and energy to make money.

Pro Tip: Extraordinary results come from doing ordinary things for an extraordinary period of time.

That's how I went from making $10,000 per month to over $1,000,000 per month. I simply got the right support, then learned the skills I needed and put them into practice every day for four years. I'm not a genius, I just have *focus*.

When I first got started in the industry and began to scale rapidly, earning my first $15,000 per month, $20,000 per month, and $30,000 per month, people that I knew had a hard time believing I was only working two to three hours a day. Sure, on a busy day I might put in an extra five hours if I needed to; or I might put in a full eight-hour day when I was working on a specific project. But for the most part, my days were fairly short in relation to how much money I was making.

My daily routine was simple: wake up, shower, eat breakfast, log into Facebook to cut spending on ads that didn't do well, and increase spending on ads that brought in lots of leads. I'd often spend half an hour writing an email to my list, which I'd schedule to go out later in the day. After that, I'd walk a couple of miles to the beach in Hawaii, hang out for an hour or so, come back for lunch, and spend the afternoon reading about sales, marketing, personal development, money, wealth, and investing.

Not a bad life, right? I learned to apply the simple concept I've shared with you throughout this book: I had decoupled my income from my time. I had learned to leverage money to make more money, not time to make more money. And as a result, I had what most people dream about: FREEDOM.

All of this is doable for you if you implement the skills you've learned. Use this book as your guide, and come back to specific chapters again and again whenever you need a refresher. If you need help implementing your sales systems and support to grow your freelance marketing business as quickly as possible, go to iiexplained.com. We can help you get everything set up in one weekend and we guarantee you results. We have the best coaches in the business to mentor and support you and powerful resources to help you succeed; and perhaps best of all, you can swipe and sell the exact same products we sell (that have produced over $120M in revenue), using the exact same sales funnels, and even copy our exact same ad strategy. This drastically reduces your learning curve so you can start seeing results almost immediately.

The key to your success is now in your hands. Once you establish your business and begin to scale, this same freedom will be yours as well.

Here's What to Do Next

Now that you know the secrets of a successful freelance marketer, there's no limit to your potential!

Reading this book is the beginning of your journey, and it's an important first step.

Here's how we can help you implement the skills you've learned and tap into our vast resources and support to help you establish and scale your business as quickly as possible.

1. Connect on Social Media

Everyday I'm sharing content to help you move forward in your life and business. You can find me here:

IG: @kealakanae
YT: @realkealakanae
TikTok: @keala_kanae
FB: Keala Kanae
X: @realkealakanae

2. Access All Your Free Bonuses

By reading this book, you've unlocked every bonus and resource my team put together to help you maximize your success.

Visit iiexplained.com to get all the extras!

About the Author

Keala Kanae is an author, entrepreneur, investor and the Founder/CEO of Fullstaq Marketer, a rapidly growing company that helps entrepreneurs build highly successful online businesses.

In August of 2012, at 29 years old, Keala gave his girlfriend (now fiancé) of 7 years a used purse his mother was dropping off at Goodwill for a friend of hers. Realizing that after 12 years of diligent work, study, and sacrifice he'd been reduced to giving someone he loved someone else's trash for her birthday, he made a solemn oath to change his and his family's future. Just a few months later, Keala quit his coffee shop job and had his first 5-figure month using the skills he shares in these pages.

Over the next 3 years, Keala earned his first million dollars as a Freelance Marketer. In late 2016, after hundreds of inquiries and requests, he launched what is now known as Fullstaq Marketer where he and his team have helped thousands of aspiring entrepreneurs launch their own online businesses. His customers come from all age brackets and all walks of life with only one thing in common: a desire to take back their financial freedom.

After creating six, seven, and even eight-figure success stories, Keala wrote *Internet Income Explained* with the hope of getting his valuable training and knowledge into more hands across the globe.

Whether he's leading his exceptionally talented Fullstaq Marketer team, spending time with his fiancé, Tiani, or visiting family in Hawaii where he was raised, Keala's focus is always on creating a greater impact in the lives he contributes to.